Produced by

10690 Los Alamitos Blvd., Los Alamitos, CA 90720
(866)252-6900 • Fax (562) 430-7877

Senior Editor
Judy Martineck

Graphic Design
Vision Marketing
Communications
Los Alamitos, California
info@visionmc.net

Thanks & Recognition

We would like to thank and recognize the companies for the use of their products throughout this book. The products and supplies that have been used and mentioned with our samples are from many different manufacturers and were picked because we believe they are products you would use. We would also like to emphasize that the mention of a product by trade name or use in this book does not constitute recommendation or endorsement for its use.

CON

Babies/Our Kids
pages 2-7

Spring
pages 8-11

Summertime
pages 12-17

Family Events/Outings
pages 18-21

Fall
pages 22-26

Winter
pages 27-29

Computer Titles
pages 30-39

Template Titles
pages 40-45

Die Cut Titles
pages 46-49

**A Little Bit of This
A Little Bit of That**
pages 50-61

**Artists
and their Tags**

Jenny Benge
pages 62-69

Linda Porter Jones
pages 70-75

Judy Martineck
pages 76-81

Jennifer Archuleta
pages 82-87

Carolyn Holt
pages 88-89

Various Artist
pages 90-96

Published by

LEISURE ARTS ®

LEISURE ARTS
5701 Ranch Drive
Little Rock, AR 72223
© 2004 by Leisure Arts, Inc.

M000105015

Bailey
by Suzee Gallagher

SUPPLIES

Background paper and Punch Outs - K & Company
Title font - Watermelon Template, Scrap Pagerz
Flower eyelets - Cut-it-Up
Chalk - Craf-T Products
Font - PC Type

Diaper
by Amber Bittenbender

Dampen square of white cardstock, crumple, wring out, using paper towels to soak up excess water. Smooth out and fold like a diaper, cutting the paper to size if necessary.
Let dry overnight or microwave for about 1 minute. Chalk if desired (Craf-T Products). Use 20 gauge wire (Darice) for pin.

Dream
by Laura Fischer

SUPPLIES

Cloud background paper - Sweetwater
Plaid paper (yellow) - The Paper Patch
Pink checked paper - Daisy D's
Dream word - Word Expressions
   by Sharon Soneff, Creative Imaginations
Star brads - Creative Imaginations
Cloud die cut - Li'l Davis
Star Punch - Emaginations
Font - CK Script
Note - Moon was designed by Laura

Scott Anthony
by Judy Martineck

SUPPLIES

Pattern paper - Over The Moon, EK Success
Vellum - Golden Oak
Sticker Letters - SEI
Threads - Two Busy Moms
Brads - Carolees
Circles - Sizzix
Font - Times New Roman

Note: I cut the white border strip 3" wide and then arranged the circles on it. Cut off the over-hanging circles with scissors. I used lined paper under the vellum as my guide for placing letters. Keep in mind some letters are taller than others.

scott anthony
born jan 17, 1986

This picture was taken at home when Scott was 3 weeks old by a professional photographer. Unlike Scott's sister who came into this world with her eyes and mouth wide open, Scott came in quiet with his eyes shut tight. He barely opened his eyes for the first 3 weeks and rarely made a peep of noise. Even when these pictures were being taken, he was not too pleased about keeping his eyes wide open.

Pixie Tag
by Judy Martineck

SUPPLIES

Pattern paper - Joni Hallmark, Creative Imaginations
Sticker - Joni Hallmark, Creative Imaginations
Font - Curlz
Thread - Magic Scrap

Tags are a great way to fill in an empty space and add journaling.

My children are like little spring pixies.
One of the delights about having a daughter was sewing her dresses.

BLOOMING BABY

Hayley and Brian have grown up so quickly! In these pictures, Brian is six months and Hayley is two...

~1994~

Blooming Baby
by Laura Fischer

SUPPLIES

Letter Stencil - 2" Whimsy, Scrap Pagerz
Wire - Westrim Crafts
Punch - Marvy Uchida
Eyelets - American Tag Co.
Font - Laura's Handwriting

3

Boys

By Judy Martineck

SUPPLIES

Background and letter paper - Carolee's Creations
Tags - American Tag Co.
Chalk - Craf-T Products
Pop Dots - All Night Media
Pen - Zig Writer, EK Success
Letters and Starbursts - Judy's design
Font - CK Stenography

Hint - There are lots of letter stencils, stickers, and/or computer fonts that can be substituted for the letters here. The tags and starbursts were chalked with blue and black.

2002 - Kyle and Scott are having fun wrestling and rough-housing. Today the only thing hurt was the furniture! Of course, the animals ran for cover!

Girls - whether big or little, just love to dress up, model or just have fun being cute!

This was in front of our house, Sarah was only 3 years old and loved to have her picture taken.

It was springtime and Mom loved to garden. So I got a shovel for myself and helped plant all the pretty flowering plants. When we were done the gardens were lovely and I was dirty!

Girls

By Judy Martineck

SUPPLIES

All pattern paper- Bryce and Madeline and Debbie Mumm, Creative Imaginations
Tags- American Tag Co.
Chalk- Craf-T Products
Pop Dots- All Night Media
Ribbon- Personal Stamp Exchange
Font- CK Journaling
Pens - Black Zig Writer, and Scroll & Brush, EK Success
Letters and Strawberries- Judy's design
Scissors - Fiskars

Delightful
by Judy Martineck

SUPPLIES

All pattern paper - Daisy D's
Vellum - Bazzill
Thread - Making Memories
Title font - CK cursive
Pen - EK Success Zig Writer
Pop Dots - All Night Media
Envelope & large flower -
    Judy's design
Fonts - CK Journaling,
CK Cursive &
Curlz MT (Microsoft Word)

Envelope
by Judy Martineck

Cut out the envelope pattern carefully. Fold in
the sides first and fold the bottom up. Use a sticker
or glue down a cut-out flower to hold folds together. Use the
envelope as your pattern for the liner, just make sure to cut it
about 1/8" smaller on all sides.

I thought I'd share the story behind these two
special pages. For those of you who have
teenagers, you will probably be able to relate
more than Mom's whose children are still young
and sweet. Anyway, I have two teenagers who
are always receiving my advise, and/or just plain
getting told what to do. Sometimes it seems,
even to me, that I'm always on my daughter's
case. So, one day out of guilt, I decided to make
a page about how special she is to me. And how
terrific she was before the days "trying to become
independent." This project was a good thing to
do for both of us.

Adorable Boy

by Judy Martineck

SUPPLIES

Star pattern paper - Cut It Up
Striped paper - Susan Branch
Gingham paper - Daisy D's
Dot pattern paper - Daisy D's
Blue Vellum - Daisy D's
Clear Vellum - Paper Garden
Thread - Making Memories
Large star - Enlargement
Solid cream - Making Memories
Envelope - Judy's design
Fonts - CK Journaling, CK Cursive & Curlz MT, MS Word

The Dancer

Sarah loves to dance and dress up as pretty as a fairy princess. This was just one of the activities that she liked to do. One moment she was clean, pretty and with that cute little girl look- and the next moment she was outside playing soccer or climbing trees with her clothes dirty and her hair a mess. Sarah loved doing anything and everything. Someday she will look at this picture and know how lucky she is to have the gift of being able to do anything.

The Dancer
by Judy Martineck

SUPPLIES

Background paper - Sonnets
   by Sharon Soneff,
   Creative Imaginations
Chalk - Craf-T Products
Font - CK Journaling
Flowers - Handmade

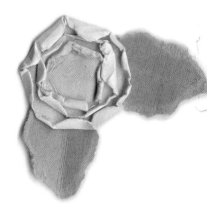

Note: Flowers are easy to make. I lightly drew a circle the size I wanted each flower and its center. Now just tear small controlled tears following the pencil lines. Curl the edges inward, then chalk using pinks, purples and blues. The leaves are made the same way.

Hearing a child's laughter warms anyone's heart. Hearing your laugh always puts a smile on my face, no matter what mood I happen to be in.

Laugh
by Amber Bittenbender

SUPPLIES

Pattern papers - Dena Designs, Creative Imaginations
Textured cardstock - NRN
Wire word - Sonnets by Sharon Soneff,
   Creative Imaginations
Fibers - Making Memories
Notes - Set eyelets on border. Run fibers from one side to the other, secure on back side. Take a small length of fibers and tie a knot off-center. Affix wire word on top.

Spring Tag
by Judy Martineck

SUPPLIES

Tag - American Tag Co.
Flower Eyelets - Cut-It-Up
Flower paper - Colors By Design
Pink plaid paper - Paper Patch
Eyelets - Creative Impressions
Twistel - Making Memories
Font - Curlz MT

Sometimes there are no words to describe what I feel when I look at your face. You have your whole life ahead of you and sometimes I worry but mostly I think you will be just fine.

Sarah
by Jennifer Archuleta

SUPPLIES

Pattern papers - Creative Imaginations
Epoxy Words - Creative Imaginations
Rub on letters and paints - Making Memories
"S" die cut letter - Twelve Timbers
Font - CK Twight
Hints - Paints are easy to use. Leave your brush dry or fairly dry. Paint lightly over all edges. When you paint one color over another, let the bottom color dry before you paint the next color on.

Even as a little girl, Sarah's personality shone brightly on her face. Whether she was happy or sad, tearful or mad, one look at her face said it all. One of the most amazing things about her is her ability to convey her feelings with just a look.

The Many Faces Of Sarah
by Jennifer Archuleta

SUPPLIES

Pattern paper - Ki Memories
Card Stock - Bazzill
Stickers & Epoxy letters - Creative Imaginations
Rafia - American Tag Co.
Buckle & flower Icicles - Ki Memories
White brads - American Tag Co.
Font - Curlz MT

"Loves Me" –Possibly the most used and most wanted phrase in our vocabulary. It brings warmth, good memories, and a smile to our hearts. I only wrote he loves me on the petals because at that age my son had lots of hugs and kisses and "I Love You's." It's one of those pictures I'd like to hang on my wall or to pull out to look at when my son is acting like a true teenager. Of course, this page layout can also be used for capturing a time between you and a parent, grandparent, husband, or boyfriend.

He Loves Me

By Judy Martineck

SUPPLIES

"Loves Me" vellum paper - Over the Moon, EK Success
Yellow Stripe pattern paper - Doodlebug
Navy paper - Pages in a Snap
Twistle - Making Memories
Lettering - Curlz, Dayco Die Cut Board
Pop Dots - All Night Media
Chalk- Craf -T Products
Flowers - Designed by Judy Martineck

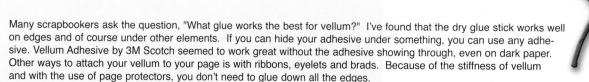

Many scrapbookers ask the question, "What glue works the best for vellum?" I've found that the dry glue stick works well on edges and of course under other elements. If you can hide your adhesive under something, you can use any adhesive. Vellum Adhesive by 3M Scotch seemed to work great without the adhesive showing through, even on dark paper. Other ways to attach your vellum to your page is with ribbons, eyelets and brads. Because of the stiffness of vellum and with the use of page protectors, you don't need to glue down all the edges.

In the past, I was reluctant about using vellum. However, that's all changed. The more I experimented and used vellum, the more I liked it. I hope you try different techniques with vellum; like tearing, layering, chalking, using eyelets, and making envelopes, just to name a few.

The Photo Shoot
by Diana Potts

SUPPLIES

Green pattern paper - Provo Craft
Eyelets - Making Memories
Flower die cuts - Accu-Cut and Dayco

Leaf die cut - Accu-Cut
Small flower punch - Family Treasures
Font- CK Curly

To Be Young

is to have

the brightness.

the innocence,

the charm,

the energy.

the sweetness,

and all the love!

Sarah
by Judy Martineck

SUPPLIES

Red Mesh - Magenta
Fibers - Fibers & Threads & Yarns,
    Oh My! A Rubba Dub Dub product
Heart die cuts - QuickKutz
Title Font - Sonja, QuickKutz
Font - CK journaling

Down by the Sea

by Cyndie Turner

SUPPLIES

Sky Paper - Carolee's Creations
Sand Paper - Wubie Prints
Title and die cuts - The Beary Patch
Pop Dots - All Night Media
Twine - unkown

Cut a couple wavy layers out of the sand paper and adhere them to the page. Cut one wavy layer out of the blue cardstock and tuck it behind the sand up against the sky background. Cut out the pieces of the Beary Patch and use pop dots behind them. When using the twine, fray the ends for a weathered look.

Water and Rope

by Judy Martineck

SUPPLIES

Water background - Paper Patch
Twine - Unknown
Vellum - Bazzill Basics Paper
Chalk - Craf-T Products

Take an 81/2 x 11 piece of white cardstock and tear all four edges. Next, with the picture that you are going to be using in the center of your page, measure out the size of the photo or just draw around the edge of the picture very lightly with a pencil. Draw an X, connecting all four corners of your box. With a craft knife, cut the two lines that make an X. Bend all four corners back, punch two holes in each flap and tie a knot with the twine. Chalk the edges as you see fit.

A Day at the Beach
by Erin Vande Lune

SUPPLIES

Beach cutouts - Cottage Quick Cuts, Keeping Memories Alive
Seashells - From the beach

Shells by Magic Scrap

Along the Sea
by Gabrielle Mader

SUPPLIES

Shell laser cuts - Deluxe Cuts

Eyelets - Impress Rubber Stamps

Along the Sea font - Lucindas Handwriting,
  Microsoft Word

Font - Lil Days

Poem - Downloaded from from Two peas in a Bucket

Just Dreamin'
By Judy Martineck

SUPPLIES

Pattern background - Sonnets by Sharon Soneff,
   Creative Imaginations
Sticker Letters - Sonnets by Sharon Soneff,
   Creative Imaginations
Brads - American Tag Co.
Chalk - Craf-T Products
Font - CK Elegant

Just about everybody has travel pictures. These two pages are fast and easy to make. If you haven't seen or used the Sonnets sticker letters by Creative Imaginations, you will be surprised. They are so precision cut with raised ink that they look like the letters are your own work of art. This is another page where vellum is used to allow the great paper to show through.

The Whole World
by Therese Mac Kendrick

SUPPLIES

World paper - Sharon Soneff, Creative Imaginations
Stitching - Sew Cute, Sewing Machine by White
Twine -Unknown
Chalk - Craf-T Products
Rectangle punch - Fiskars
Font - Garamond (Microsoft Word)

Tiny Bubbles

by Linda Smith

SUPPLIES

Background paper - SEI
Bubble Stickers - Creative Imaginations
Die Cut Letters - Unknown
Bubble bottle and wand die cut - Stamping Station
Computer Font - DJ Script

Sticker by Creative
Imaginations

Chalk It Up

by Linda Smith

SUPPLIES

Background paper - Renae Lindgren
    Cardstock, Creative Imaginations
Chalk Border - Shotz, Creative Imaginations
Cardstock - The Perfect Scrapbook, ColorBok
Die Cut Letters - Ignacio
Computer Font - Unknown

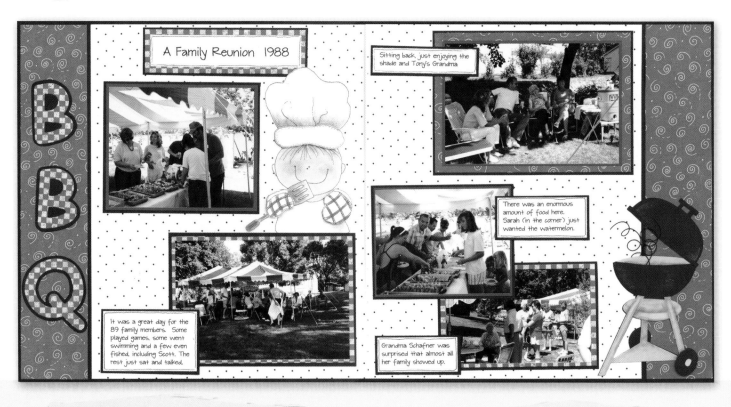

BBQ by Judy Martineck

SUPPLIES

Black dot paper - Mary Englebrich, Creative Imaginations
Red swirl and red check paper - Ever After
Flat silver metallic paper - Hot off the Press
Chef - Luv Bugz, Puzzlemates
BBQ die cut - Ellison
Letter die cuts - Dayco
Chalk - Craf-T Products
Pop Dots - All Night Media

This page is fairly simple and is easily altered to accommodate what supplies and pictures you have. The BBQ title can be made from any 2" letter stencil and then your own cut black background letters. The barbecue is a little more difficult. Using the picture and two barbecue die cuts, just cut and paste. The smoke can be made with either wire or very thin cuts of black paper.

Happy 4th of July

by Rhiana Desuacido

SUPPLIES

Red and Navy cardstock - Renae Lindgren,
   Creative Imaginations
Pattern paper - Renae Lindgren
   Creative Imaginations
Star eyelets - Doodlebug Designs
Sticker letters - David Walker, Colorbok
Micro glass beads - Craftware
Patriotic beads - Magic Scraps
Shaker box - Rhiana's own design
Font - Kristen ITC
Hint - Stars are cut from Renae Lindgren paper

The day before the 4th of July, Scott's preschool celebrated by spending the day at Green Valley Farm. This was a petting farm so the kids got to touch or pet many animals.

The lambs were fun. I think Scott preferred the back end more than the head.

The turkeys were definitely a different story. They were loud and scarey, and would peck at the kids.

Scott was afraid at first to ride the pony. By the second slap, he was smiling.

Patriotic Boy
By Judy Martineck

SUPPLIES

Star-Pattern background - Sweetwater
Patriotic boy - Luv Bugz, Puzzle Mates
Star die cut - Ellison; Star punch - Emagination
Pop Dots - All Night Media
Chalk - Craf-T Products
Brads - American Tag Co.
Wire - Westrim Crafts
Flag - Designed by Judy Martineck
Font - CK Journaling

My Little Star

Just another one of those wonderful days watching Scott's face beamed with excitement and happiness.

Snips & Snails!

and lots of Smiles!

My Little Star
By Judy Martineck

SUPPLIES

Pattern paper - NRN Designs
Star die cut - Ellison
Eyelets - Creative Impressions
Wire - Westrim Crafts
Pop Dots - All Night Media
Fonts - CurlzMT, Microsoft Word; DJ Doodlers, DJ Inkers
Pen - Zig Writer, EK Success
Chalk - Craf-T Products

Sidewalk Stars

by Linda Jones

SUPPLIES

Background paper - SEI
Star stickers - Mrs. Grossman's
Title letter stencil - Deja Views
Pen - Zig writer, EK Success
Chalk - Craf-T Products

Wire - Westrim
Star punch - Family Treasures
Corner Rounder - Scrap Artistry
Star Stickers - Mrs. Grossman's

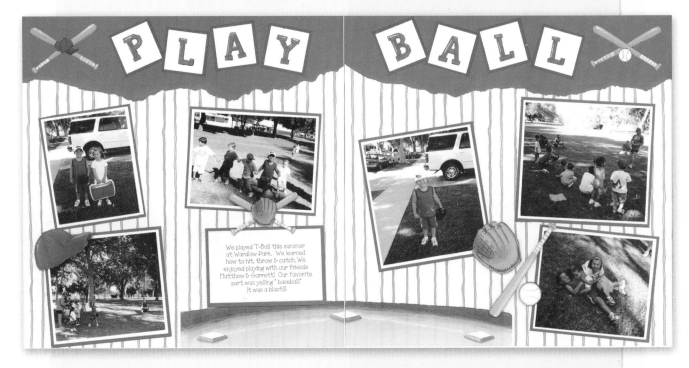

Play Ball

by Linda Smith

SUPPLIES

Background paper - Printworks
Stickers - Karen Foster
Font - DJ Goo

Auto Shop 101

by Laura Fischer

SUPPLIES

Magic Mesh - Avant Card
Washers - Creative Impressions
Dotlets - Doodlebug Designs

Eyelets - Cut-it-Up
Title template - Chunky College Scrap Pagerz
Font - CK Toggle and CK Fill In
Pen - Zig Writer, EK Success

Dice by
Creative Imaginations

Dice

by Shoshana Yudin

SUPPLIES

Title - Griffs shortcuts

To make dice, cut squares and round the corners using a corner rounder (Marvy). Punch (EK Success) out circles and place them on the rounded squares, to make them look like dice. Place the dice along the edges of the page to make a border. Place a picture in the center of the layout.

We love making the annual trek to the Tall Ship Festival. Lots of vendors and activities make for a fun, festive and pirate filled atmosphere. The smell of Kettle corn gets us through the crowd and rewards us with a warm, sweet and salty treat! The wait in line is worth it when the kids get to explore 3 huge sailing ships to their hearts' content.

Dana Harbor

Tall Ships
by Allison Bergquist

SUPPLIES

Template - All-In-One, Puzzlemates
Cutouts - Beary Patch
Sticker letters - Pathways, Provo Craft
Cardstock - Two toned, Paper Adventures

I'm Wild About…
by Gabrielle Mader

SUPPLIES

Sticker letters - Mary Engelbriet,
   Creative Imginations
Black Mesh - Magenta
Wild font - Unknown
Small envelope - Impress Rubber Stamps

Black gingham ribbon - Offray
Wire - Westrim Crafts
Alphabet beads - Westrim Crafts
Leopard ribbon- Unknown
Tags- Unkown; Font - Unknown

The San Diego Zoo

What do you do when you go to the Zoo?
Do you hippity-hop like a gray kangaroo?
Do you roar like a big heavy lion would do?
Is that what you do when you go to the Zoo?

What do you do when you go to the Zoo?
Do you say to the elephant, "how do you do?"
Do you watch all the monkeys while they're watching you?
Is that what you do when you go to the Zoo?

What do you do when you go to the Zoo?
Do you count if the camel has one hump or two?
Do you find the giraffe and see how tall he grew?
There's so much to do when you go to the Zoo!

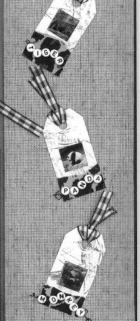

Going Wild
by Linda Smith

SUPPLIES

Animal pattern paper - Making Memories
Going Wild Title - My Minds Eye
Frames - My Minds Eye
Safari kid die cut - My Minds Eye
Animal die cuts - Stamping Station

Copper background - NRN Designs
Twine - Unknown
Font - DJ Desert
Eyelets - American Tag Co.
Map - From the zoo they visited

Zoo
By Judy Martineck

SUPPLIES

Small dot background paper, Mary Engelbriet
  Creative Imaginations
Big Dot paper (yellow) - Chatterbox, EK Success
Stripes paper (yellow) - Chatterbox, EK Success
Brown Twistel - Making Memories
Eyelets - American Tag
Wire - Westrim Crafts
Chalk - Craf-T Products
Pop Dots - All Night Media

Hints - The letters "ZOO" were Judy's own design. They can easily be substituted with any stencil or computer font that you like. White cardstock was used and chalked the desired color. The spots were drawn and all the pen detail was done before chalking. Two pieces of Twistel were used to hang the letters. Tie a knot at one end of both pieces of Twistel. Then thread one through the hole at the top of the first "O"and the other end over the bottom of the "Z." Use the same procedure for attaching the two "O's." Tombo Multi Purpose glue was used to attach the Twistel. Vellum can be used with most printers, just allow a few minutes for the ink to dry before tearing or chalking the edges.

The Magic Kingdom

by Amber Bittenbender

SUPPLIES

Black ribbed cardstock - NRN
Stickers - Sandylion
Title letters - Mt. Range template,
   Scrap Pagerz
Font - Pristina, Microsoft Word
Brads - 3/16" Carolees Creations &
   1/8" Karen Foster for tiny Mickey

Hint: Extend and slightly widen the
   bottom of the first three letters.
   Then place the first three letters
   on top of black paper and the
   rest on white paper, and then
   cut your 1/16" backing.

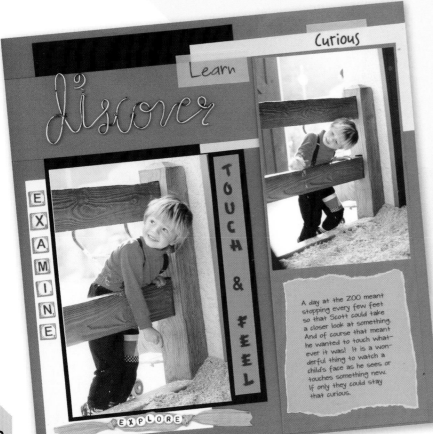

Discover

by Judy Martineck

SUPPLIES

Title discover - Wire Expressions by
   Sharon Soneff, Creative Imaginations
Twistel - Making Memories
Letter Beads - Westrim crafts
Fonts - CK Journaling, Easy Goin',
   Footnote, Game Night and Paintbrush

Goin' Goofy
by Laura Tebbetts

SUPPLIES

Pattern paper - Over the Moon,
   EK Success
Swirl punch - Family Treasures

Going Goofy title - Cock-a-Doodle
Goofy die cuts - Cock-a-Doodle
Font - DJ Crayon

A Very Goofy Day
by Amber Bittenbender

SUPPLIES

Background pattern paper - Scrapbook Wizard
Stickers - Sandylion
Swirl Charms - Carolees Creations
Brads - Karen Foster
Font - Microsoft Word
Hint: Place charms where you would like them,
   pierce a hole and then put the brad
   through the charm and hole.

It's Fall Fun Time
by Judy Martineck

SUPPLIES

Straw border - Shotz, Creative Imaginations

Brads - American Tag Co.

Computer font - Curlz MT, Microsoft Word

Hint - Cut picture into three strips, with the ends smaller than the middle, then mount them on your cardstock spacing them evenly.

It's Such Fun
by Judy Martineck

SUPPLIES

Leaves sticker - Provo Craft
Font - Curlz MT, Microsoft Word
Trash can - Judy's own design
Chalk - Craf-T Products
Hint - I mounted the leaves around the trash can on white cardstock, then I used an Exacto knife to start the cutting around the leaves and small scissors where they would fit.

Barrel of Leaves
by Amber Bittenbender

SUPPLIES

Barrel - Deluxe Cuts
Leaves sticker - Provo Craft
Rivets - American Tag Co.
Chalk - Craf-T Products
Hint - Mount leaves on cardstock and then cut out.

Fall Leaves Me Happy

by Linda Jones

SUPPLIES
Leaf vellum - K and Company
Title font - Pebble in My Pocket
Eyelets - Creative Impressions
Leaf pattern - Linda's Design

Pen - Zig writer, EK Success
Twine - Unknown
Chalk - Craf-T Products

Pumpkin Patch

by Sandra Ott

SUPPLIES
Orange pattern paper - Pages in a Snap,
   Two Busy Moms
Eyelets - Creative Impressions
String - Stitches, Making Memories
Twistel - Making Memories
Pen - Zig writer, EK Success

Title font - Wacky Letters, Die Cuts "R" Us
Pumpkin and Scarecrow patterns -
   Annie Langs 201 Paper Piecing pattern,
   Hot of the Press
Font- DJ Squirrely
Twine- Unknown

Will Spook for Treats
by Gabrielle Mader

SUPPLIES

Purple background paper -
    Doodlebug Design Inc.
Black plaid paper - Keeping Memories Alive
Eyelets - Doodlebug Designs, Inc.
Tags - American Tag Co.
Sticker Letters - David Walker, Colorbok
Laser Cut - Deluxe Cuts
Fibers - Magic Scraps
Font- Garamouche, Impress Rubber Stamps

Cinderella's Pumpkin Patch
by Gabrielle Mader

SUPPLIES
Background paper - Provo Craft
Sticker letters - David Walker, Colorbok
Eyelets - Impress Rubber Stamps
Fence - Unknown
Tags - Gabrielle's design
Pumpkins - Gabrielle's design
Wooden stars - Unknown
Tag Idea - Kopps Klip Its

Trick or Treat

by Laura Fischer

SUPPLIES

Orange pattern - Making Memories
Jack-o-Lantern punch - Family Treasures
Orange washers - Creative Impressions
Black eyelets - Creative Impressions

Title font - Deja Views
Font - CK Journaling
String- Making Memories

Scary Night

by Judy Martineck

SUPPLIES

Black Mesh - Magenta Style
Purple pattern paper - Ever After
Letter Template - Scrap Pagerz
Halloween Ribbon - Unknown
Ghosts - pattern from ribbon
Pen - Zig writer, EK Success
Font - Comic Sans, Microsoft Word

Cherry Pickin'
by Linda Jones

SUPPLIES

Cherry pattern paper - Mary Engelbreit, Creative Imaginations
Green and Burgundy pattern paper - Making Memories
String - Unknown

Pen - Zig Writer, EK Success
Cherry die cut - Mary Engelbreit, Creative Imaginations
Metallic Rub on - Craf-T Products

Park Birthday
by Linda Smith

SUPPLIES

Background paper - NRN Designs; Park letters - Template, Deja Views
Birthday letters - Unkown
Font - DJ Senf

Best Time of the Year Tag

SUPPLIES

Gold paper - Paper Co.

Green handmade paper - Maruyama, Magenta

Fibers- Fibers & Threads & Yarn, Oh My,
   (a Rubba Dub Dub product)

Gold metallic rub-on - Craft-T Products

Font - Curlz MT (Microsoft Word)

Threads (center flower) - Unknown

Ribbon - Unknown

Christmas 1986

by Judy Martineck

SUPPLIES

Background paper - Anna Griffin
Christmas ribbon - Holiday Accents,
   Hirschberg Schultz & Co., Inc.
Eyelets - American Tag Co.
Red cording - Unknown;   Fonts - CK Journaling

A Merry Christmas

by Amber Bittenbender

SUPPLIES

Background Sand krinkle pattern - Creative Imaginations; Letter stickers - Martin Brush, Creative Imaginations; Metallic Gold Stripe (presents) - Paper Pizzaz; Gold star - Carolee's Creations; Gold brad - American Tag Co.; Ribbons & Twine - local store Gold & silver cord - Printworks; Beads - Art Accentz ; Present die cut - QuickKutz Holly die cut - Accu/Cut

Snow Angel
by Laura Tebbetts

SUPPLIES

Snowflake paper- Cut-it-Up
Key tags- Unknown
Silver eyelets- Creative Impressions
Snowflake eyelets- The Stamp Dr.
Wire- Westrim Crafts
Circle punch- Family Treasures
Sticker letters- Me and My Big Ideas
Font- Unknown

"Emily had the best time in the snow this year! She went sledding, built a snowman, and enjoyed playing in the snow. She is our little "Snow Angel."

March 2002

Winter Tag
by Judy Martineck

I glued background paper (Sonnets, Creative Imagination) to tag (American Tag Co) Then cut 3 - 1" squares (clear vellum and 2 Maruyama papers by Magenta). Place them on tag as if to make a large square. Leave enough space in between the 1" squares for the thread. Lay the thread on the tag where it's suppose to be and make a small notch at the edge of the tag where the thread wraps around to the back. This will hold the thread in place. Tape down the thread on the back. Winter was embossed (Lasting Impressions) and chalked (Craf-T Products). Extreme Eyelet - Creative Imaginations.

Mammoth 2001
We had one of the best trips to Mammoth this year! There was lots of snow and not a lot of people around, so we had the mountain all to ourselves most of the time!

Winter Snow
by Shauna Boyd

SUPPLIES

All pattern paper - Renae Lindgren,
   Creative Imaginations
Punchouts - Renae Lindgren,
   Creative Imagination
Clear vellum - Golden Oaks
Font - CK Inky

The Christmas Boat Parade
by Suzee Gallagher

SUPPLIES

Background paper - Over the Moon Press,
 EK Success
Silver ribbon - Unknown
Silver embossing powder - The Stamp Inn
Snowflake charms - Magic Scraps
Snowflake laser cuts - Deluxe Cuts
Rhinestones - Unknown
Blue denim paper - Debbie Mumm,
 Creative Imaginations
Beads - Unknown
Fonts - Palace Script

Let It Snow
by Judy Martineck

SUPPLIES

Background paper - Sandylion
Clear Vellum - Golden Oaks
Laser Snowflakes - Deluxe Die Cuts
Snowflake Eyelets - Carolees
Snow letters - Script, Scrap pagerz
Pop Dots - All Night Media
Font - Lucida Handwriting
Note: Vellum swirls hand drawn and cut
    out. Vellum Adhesive by Scotch was
    cut in thin strips for swirls and "Let It",
    and used full size under journaling
    (just remember to press all of the
    adhesive into the paper before apply-
    ing the vellum). Pop Dots were also
    cut very thin strips for snowflakes.

"The Computer" Title

Making a computer generated title is my favorite method for my titles. The computer pretty much doesn't limit my desire or ability. The words I choose for my title can be as long or short as I like and I can create the font size that is perfect for the space on my page. Whatever color or style of font I prefer, it's possible with just the touch of the finger. Furthermore, I can print the title on any background paper of my choice. As you look at the titles in this section, I think you will find that most of the titles were printed on clear vellum. Printing on clear vellum lends to the ease of matching your title to any color theme on your page layout. This can be very convenient, especially if you would like to do your journaling while it's fresh in your mind or if you just want to be prepared ahead of time for a crop you're going to.

If you haven't used vellum before, it is fairly easy to work with. It can be printed on with either a laser printer or an inkjet printer. With the inkjet printer, you need to let the ink dry for a minute or two. Vellum can be attached to your page by several different methods. When using adhesives, the best method is to place the adhesive under an element so it won't show. This method allows you to use any adhesive. When you are using vellum for journaling, the best adhesive is one that will not show even on a dark color paper. Scotch Vellum Tape works great if you apply it according to the directions. You only need to put a strip of tape in one or two spots under the writing depending on the size of your vellum. The Xyron is also great for attaching the whole piece of vellum. Other effective methods of attaching vellum are using brads, eyelets and ribbons.

As you make or experiment with making your own computer title, try some of the other techniques used in this section. Adding pen lines and chalking can create a whole new look. Tearing the edges is also a great effect. All of these techniques are easy to do on both cardstock and vellum.

Vanessa and I were best friends in 8th grade, had slumber parties, spent an endless amount of time on the phone, passed countless notes in class and laughed for hours.

Flower Power Girl Power
Hangin' after school
Getting crazy with a friend
Acting oh so cool
This is what life's about
Pink and all that stuff
It's so fun to be a girl
We can't get enough!

Laura Fischer
Vanessa McCall

St. Hedwig School
June 1996

Forever Friends
by Judy Martineck

SUPPLIES

Title fonts - Beesknees ITC and
   CK Quake
Papers - SanLori Designs
Wire - Westrim Craft
Pen - Zig Writer, EK Success
Pop Dots - All Night Media
Poems - Tiny tales, My Minds Eyes
Hints - The color I clicked on for the letters Forever, which was the bright green under Microsoft Word, just happen to match perfectly. I attached the wire with a very small piece of the thin wire placed through two needle holes.

Staying Cool
by Judy Martineck

SUPPLIES

Font - CK Journaling
Pattern paper - Colors by Design
Blue vellum - Hot Off The Press
Cardstock - Bazzill Basics Paper
Wire - Westrim Crafts
Silver drops - Scrap Yard
Hose pattern - Judy's own design
Vellum - Bazzill Basics Paper
Yellow Brads - Ting-A-Lings, Carolees Creations
Chalk - Craf-T Products
Title Font - CK Broad Pen and CK Paintbrush

A hot summer late afternoon in 1987 on the sidewalk in front of our house - Scott was about 20 months old when the sensation of touching, feeling and having new experiences were still thrilling to a child. Something as simple as just watching the water trickle out of the sprinkler head made him giggle.

Both these pages demonstrate the use of chalk and creating pen lines. If you're going to create a title with both techniques, make your pen lines first. Chalking doesn't have to be perfect. Just pick a color from your paper or picture and blend the chalk around the edges.

A "Tom Sawyer" Picnic
by Judy Martineck

SUPPLIES

Font - CK Storybook
Background paper - Scrapbook Sally
Cardstock - Bazzill Basics Paper and Colorbok
Fibers - Scrapbook Sally
Butterflies and Brads - Ting-A-Lings, Carolees Creations
Pen - Zig Writer, EK Success
Chalk - Craf-T Products
Pop Dots - All Night Media

Even for little girls dressing in overalls, putting on a favorite hat, wrapping a picnic lunch in a large scarf and tying it to a stick was a wonderful adventure! Down to the park we would walk. Sometimes we would sit out in the open, and sometimes we would pretend to be like Tom Sawyer and hide. But we always had so much fun at our park.

It was spring time, 1988 and Sarah was just 4!

Gingham Pocket
by Amber Bittenbender

SUPPLIES
Plaid paper - Daisy D's; Buttons - Making Memories
Cardstock - Monochromatics, Bazzill Basics Paper
Flower die cuts - QuicKutz
Eyelets and snaps - Making Memories
White pen - Marvy Uchida
Rivets - American Tag

Sarah would pick flowers when ever she wasn't doing anything else. Sometimes it was a daily thing. The flowers in the back yard were, at times, gone from being all picked by Sarah. Unfortunately, Sarah went picking flowers from our neighbor's until I caught her. She just loved flowers and thought they were free for the picking.

My Flower Girl
by Judy Martineck

SUPPLIES
Background paper - Cut-it-Up; Cardstock - Bazzill Basics Paper; Stitching - As You Wish, (Sewing Machine); Jean Pocket - Designed by Amber Bittenbender; Flower and Leaf die cuts - QuicKutz; Pen - Zig Writer, EK Success; Font - Gigi, Microsoft Word

Our kiddos having some...
GOOD
CLEAN
FUN

In August, when we took our trip without Daddy to Bakersfield, you and Victoria and Bella shared a bath and had the most fun! You guys were beyond silly and had soap bubbles flying everywhere! (Cameron was too little to get in with you; that is why he is not in the picture). But the three of you had a crazy time putting bubbles on each other's heads and splashing around. After the bath, you all played in the spray of the shower and that's when we got the tushy shot. I hope when you get older you don't think I'm horrible for that picture!! It was such fun.

Victoria   Zachary   Isabella

Good Clean Fun
by Jennifer Archuleta

SUPPLIES
Cardstock & Vellum - Bazzill Basics Paper; Circle die cuts - Sizzix; Stickers - Penny Black; Paper Eyelets - Making Memories; Twistel - Making Memories; Brads - Ting-A-Lings, Carolees Creations; Splash die cuts- Ellison; Vellum tags - Making Memories; Colored Pencils - Prang; Fonts- CK Sink or Swim and CK Easy Going.

In the eyes of a child...

By Amber Bittenbender

SUPPLIES

Cardstock - Monochromatics, Bazzill Basics Paper
Vellum - The Paper Company
Punch-outs and stickers - Renae Lindgren,
    Creative Imaginations
Blue Fibers - Creative Imaginations
Yellow Fibers - Adornaments, EK Success
Pocket Template - Deluxe Cuts
Nails - Scrapbook Interiors, Chatterbox
Micro beads - Magic Scraps
Font - Edwardian Script ITC

Hints - To make the title, first glue the three colored cardstocks together with a temporary adhesive (Hermafix removable). Cut the cardstock so that it is about 2 inches larger than the desired finished size - making it easier to tear. Now, tear through all three sheets on one long side and one short side. Take small, slightly controlled tears with your right hand, using your left thumb to control the tearing. After you have torn the first two sides, move the middle paper about 3/4 of an inch down and over, the top paper about 1 inch down and over. The top papers should overlap two sides of the bottom paper. After tearing the two remaining sides, move the layers so they are centered and secure using an adhesive. Measure the size of your title after tearing and use this measurement as a guideline when typing your text. Choose your font, and print it on vellum. After allowing the ink to dry, cut the vellum to size using a paper trimmer, scissors or the tearing technique used above. Next, glue the vellum down. Amber used the Xyron Sticker Maker on the vellum, but any adhesive can be used if it is under the area of the flowers or any other element. Glue the flowers in place and then punch a 1/16 inch hole through the centers and attach the nails. After the flower stickers are put on the tags, dot on small amounts of Mono Multi Glue wherever the micro-beads are desired. When the glue has completely dried, press the tag into the micro-beads (use a bead tray or shallow dish to hold the beads in). The threads for the tags were folded in half, pulled through the hole, and then pulled through the looped end.

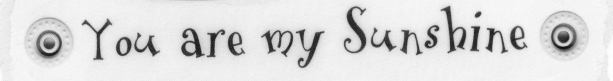

You are my Sunshine

by Judy Martineck

SUPPLIES

Cardstock & Vellum - Bazzil Basics Paper;
Rivets - Scrapbook Interiors, Chatterbox; Font - CK Fantasy

Up, Up, and Away
by Laura Archuleta

SUPPLIES
Background Paper - Paper Patch; Cardstock - Bazzill Basics Paper;
Fibers - EK Success Adornaments; Title Font - Tweed-Internet,
moms Corner4kids.com; Font - PC Lorisans

Beauty and the Beach
by Jennifer Archuleta

SUPPLIES Cardstock- Bazzill Basics Paper; Vellum - Bazzill Basics Paper;
Fibers - Magic Scraps; Letters and Word Snaps - Making Memories; Metal Frame - Making Memories;
Eyelets - American Tag Co.; Chalk - Craf-T Products; Title Fonts - CK Bella & CK Journaling; Font - CK Journaling

The simplicity of these layouts is due to the fact that the designers wanted to include quite a few photographs on the pages. All of the embellishments are along the periphery of the layouts to showcase what is most important - the photographs themselves.

What it's like to be...

by Jennifer Archuleta

SUPPLIES

Fonts - PC Lorisans
Cardstock- Bazzill Basics Paper
Vellum envelope - Tid-Bits, Deja Views
Vellum Tag - Making Memories
Vellum - Bazzill Basics Paper
Brads - Creative Impressions
Twine - Local Craft Store

Designing a page that lists the attributes that make your child special is a way to forever freeze in time the unique personality he possesses at that age. As he grows, matures and changes, you will always be able to look back at the sweet child he once was.

What it's like to be Sisters

by Judy Martineck

SUPPLIES

Title Font - CK Serendipity
Journaling Font - CK Tea Party
Cardstock & vellum - Bazzill Basics Paper

Frame hint - Place picture on paper, draw pencil line around picture. Tear edges about 1/2" from line. Poke a hole in the center with your scissors, then cut from center to just short of each corner. Now tear from corner to corner an arch. Fold each arch out, back and out again; if you have too much paper left, tear more off. Take the torn off pieces and cut the side that is not torn so that the width is 1/4". Now roll into a flower. Tear leaves and fold.

Daddy, Dad, Father
By Dana Hauser

SUPPLIES

Cardstock - Bazzill Basics Paper
Handmade paper - Umbria, Pulsar Paper
Pattern paper - The Paper Patch
Font - CK Constitution, CK Elusive,
    CK Stenography, Centaur Italic
Twistel - Making Memories
Star Accents - Ting-A-Lings, Carolees Creations
Chalks - Craf-T Products
Buttons - Local Craft Store
Black eyelets - Making Memories
Small star punch - Family Treasures

Thanksgiving Border
by Judy Martineck

SUPPLIES

Fall Leaves - Leaf, Oak #2 Small, Accu Cut
Vellum Paper - Bazzill Basics Paper
Eyelets - American Tag Co.; Wire - Westrim Crafts
Chalk - Craf-T Products; Font - DJ Sketched

My Husband... My Best Friend
by Jennifer Archuleta

SUPPLIES

Title Font and journaling - Anna Plain,
    CK Bella, DJ Sketched
Cardstock - SEI
Vellum - WorldWin
Mulbery (black) - Bazzill Basic Paper
Charm - Making Memories
Fibers - Making Memories Stitches

The Sport of Paintballing
by Judy Martineck

SUPPLIES

Camouflage paper - Making Memories
Cardstock - Bazzill Basics Paper
Army man laser cut - Deluxe Cuts
Splats - Judy's own design
Paintball gun - Judy's own design
Chalk - Craf-T Products
Title fonts - CK Journaling and CK Paintbrush
Font - CK Journaling

Stickers -
Karen Foster Design

We love our Troops
by Shana Yudin

SUPPLIES

Handmade mesh paper - Creative Imaginations; Bamboo vellum - Golden Oak; Tag template - Deluxe Cuts; Camouflage paper - Creative Imaginations; Cardstock - Bazzill Basics Paper; India silver paper - The Paper Company; Wire - Westrim Crafts; Eyelets - American Tag Co.; Sticker letters - Making Memories; Star punch - All Night Media; Flag - Shana's own design; Pen - Zig Writer, EK Success; Chalk - Craf-T Products; Title font - Khaki, QuicKutz; Font - CK Stenography

My Father
by Judy Martineck

SUPPLIES
Pattern paper- Doodlebug Designs
Cardstock and vellum - Bazzill Basics Paper
Tie papers - The Paper Company,
    Printworks and Sue Dreamer, Colorbok
Tie pattern - Judy's own design
Chalk - Craf-T products
Wire - Westrim Crafts
Pen - Zig Writer, EK Success
Font - CK Cursive
Hint - White cord was a shoestring, however,
it could be substituted with a strip of white paper
or even ribbon.

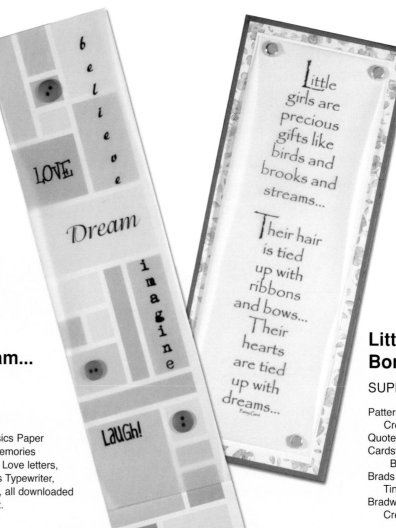

Love, Dream...
by Linda Jones

SUPPLIES

Pattern paper - SEI
Vellum - Bazzill Basics Paper
Buttons - Making Memories
Font - Brush455BT, Love letters,
    Adorable, Mom's Typewriter,
    and Genericfont, all downloaded
    from the internet.

Little Girls Border

SUPPLIES

Pattern paper - Dena Desig
    Creative Imaginations
Quote - Quick Quotes
Cardstock - Bazzill
    Basics Paper
Brads - Carolees Creations
    Ting-A-Lings
Bradwear -   Impress-ons,
    Creative Imaginations

I Thee Wed...
by Laura Fischer

SUPPLIES

Pattern paper - Dena Designs, Creative Imaginations
Tag - Rebecca Sower Fresh Tags, EK Success
Dove stickers - Jolee's Boutique, EK Success
Flower punch - Family Treasures
Font - CK Script
Wire and jewels - Westrim Crafts

Hint - The bouquet of flowers was made by punching the little flowers and gluing rhinestones in the center of each flower. Then glue the cardstock stems down and add flowers. Next punch a tiny hole on either side of the stems using a heavy needle or 1/16" hole punch. Cut a piece of wire about 9-12inches and pull through the holes. Twist the wire to form a bow, trimming the ends to desired length.

Sometimes stepping away from your own photographs and entrusting them into another's care is the best way to overcome scrapper's block. A friend will most likely see your photographs from an entirely different perspective than you do. When Laura went through the bride's photographs, she immediately saw the first photograph as the perfect beginning of Erin's album and the second photograph as the perfect end to her fairy tale day…

And They Lived
Happily Ever After
by Laura Fischer

SUPPLIES

Pattern paper - Dena Designs, Creative Imaginations
Cardstock and vellum - Bazzill Basics Paper
Dove stickers - Jolee's Boutique, EK Success
Flower punch - Family Treasures
Wire and Jewels - Westrim Crafts
Font - CK Script

39

Templates

According to template enthusiasts, letter templates are the most versatile and fun way to create titles. These wonderful templates have been manufactured in many shapes, sizes and styles. They are inexpensive, easy to store and come in many different variations for any given event. Lettering templates have a way of making every page in an album unique. You can experiment with creating different shadow effects, you can turn a letter into an object or a shape that reflects the event, and you can make your letters different colors to match the color scheme of your layout. You might even try using chalk and pen lines for a dramatic look. Whatever you do, letter templates always seem to add that extra flair to your page.

In this section we're trying to demonstrate not only different letter techniques, but also different title placements. The most frequently used placement of a title is at the top of the page. A slight variation of this placement would be to split the title, placing part at the top and part in the middle or at the bottom of the next page. Before you glue your title on the page, move it around on your page or pages to create a few different effects and then choose which placement best suites the flow and the feeling of the page.

School
by Judy Martineck

SUPPLIES
Lettering Template - Whimsy, Scrap Pagerz; Pattern paper - Over the Moon Press, EK Success; Chalk - Chalklets EK Success; Pens - Zig Writer (Black), Zig Scroll and Brush (Platinum), EK Success and Gel Excel (White), Marvy; Pencils - Rebecca Sower Fresh Sticker, EK Success.

Hints - Trace your letters reverse on the backside of the paper so you don't need to erase the lines. I cut these letters out a little fatter and when I made an error cutting off the lines, I just continued cutting to keep the cut smooth. After gluing the letters down, I created the shadow with the platinum brush pen. Place the pointed tip on the background paper next to the edge at the top of the letter. Press down on the pen as you move down the letter and lift up where you want it thinner. Practice on the backside of a letter or a scrap piece of paper. It is easy! This shadowing gives a raised look without the thickness. For the O (apples) - cut the stem and leaves, draw black lines, chalk, and make the white highlight.

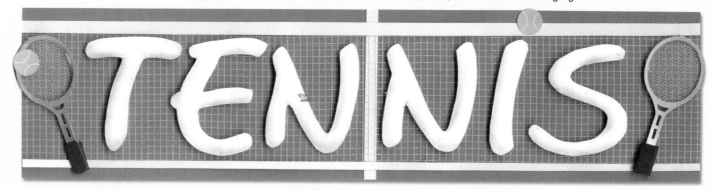

Tennis
by Judy Martineck

SUPPLIES
Lettering Templates - Script, Scrap Pagerz; Cardstock - Bazzill Basics Paper; Netting - Magic Mesh; Tennis embellishments - Jolee's by You, EK Success; Pop Dots - All Night Media; Chalk - Craf-T Products

My 21st Birthday

by Laura Fischer

SUPPLIES

Lettering Template - Script, Scrap Pagerz; Silver paper - India Silver, The Paper Company;
Red handmade paper - Maruyama, Magenta; Cardstock and vellum - Bazzill Basics Paper;
Star brads - Creative Imaginations; Small brads - American Tag Co.; Wire - Westrim Crafts;
Square and star punches - Family Treasures; Font – Kristen ITC

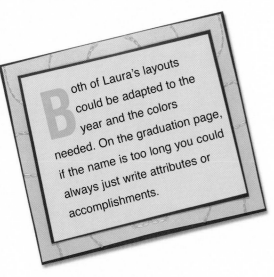

Both of Laura's layouts could be adapted to the year and the colors needed. On the graduation page, if the name is too long you could always just write attributes or accomplishments.

Class of 2000

by Laura Fischer

Lettering Template - EK Success
Yellow stitched paper - Creative
   Imaginations
Cardstock and Vellum - Bazzill
   Basics Papers
Fibers - Adornaments,
   EK Success
Washers - Creative Impressions
Fonts - CK Handprint

41

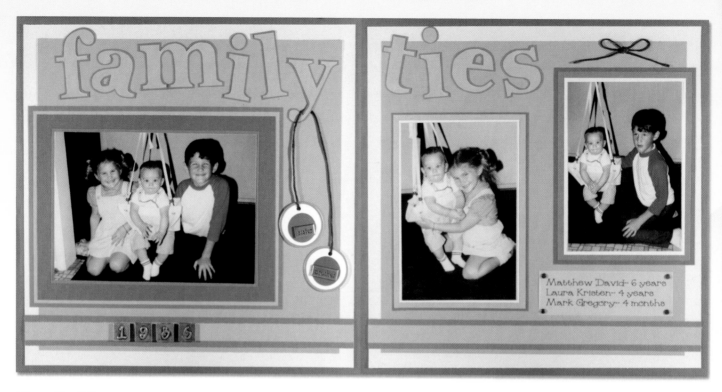

Family Ties
by Laura Fischer

SUPPLIES

Lettering Template - Typewriter, Scrap Pagerz; Cardstock and vellum - Bazzill Basics Paper; Brads - American Tag Co.; Fiber - Waxy Flax, Scrapworks; Eyelet words - Making Memories; Tag Wear - Impress-ons, Creative Imaginations; Round tags - American Tag Co.; Savvy Tiles - Creative Imaginations; Font - DJ Serif

Summer
by Judy Martineck

SUPPLIES

Lettering Template - Curly Q, Scrap Pagerz
June paper - Sweetwater
Cardstock & vellum - Monochromatic,
    Bazzill Basics Paper
Buttons - Making Memories
Fibers - Creative Imaginations
Pen - Zig Writer, EK Success
Chalk - Craf-T Products
Daisy Die Cuts - Judy's own design,
    inspired by the background paper
Font - CK Journaling

I Wish to be a FISH
by Linda Jones

SUPPLIES

Title and Fish paper piecing
    swap from Angelia Wigginton
Paper - SEI
Cardstock and vellum - Bazzill Basics Paper
Fibers - Stitches, Making Memories and Adornaments,
    EK Success
Glitter - Magic Scraps
Small eyelets - Doodlebug Design
Large eyelets - American Tag Co.
Pen - Zig Writer, EK Success
Font - downloaded from the internet

Such Goofy Boys
by Linda Jones
SUPPLIES

Letter Template – Party, Scrap Pagerz
Cardstock - Bazzill Basics Paper
Pen – Zig Writer, EK Success
Font - Linda's own handwriting

BOY Stuff
by Judy Martineck

SUPPLIES

Letter template -
    Mt. Range, ScrapPagerz
Cardstock -
    Bazzill Basic Papers
Large tag -
    Fresh Tags, EK Success
Small tag punch -
    Emaginations
Font -
    CK Teacher's Pet
Baseball items -
    Jolee by You,
    EK Success
Car - ProvoCraft
Lizard - QuicKutz
Chalk - Craf-T Products
Pen - Black Zig Writer,
    EK Success
Jute - Local store

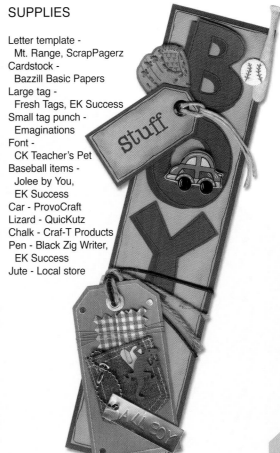

43

It's spring so "BEE" happy
by Linda Jones

SUPPLIES
Lettering Template - Script, Scrap Pagerz; Flower die cuts - Linda's design;
Cardstock and vellum - Bazzill Basics Paper; Bee die cut - Linda's design; Wire - Westrim Craft;
Pen - Zig Writer, EK Success; Title font - Kristen ITC; Font - Linda's own handwriting

Friends Forever
by Linda Jones

SUPPLIES   Letter Template - Script, Scrap Pagerz; Background paper - Daisy D's; Cardstock - Bazzill Basics Paper; Tags - American Tag Co.;
Sticker letters - Mary Engelbriet, Creative Imaginations; Buttons - Local craft store; Flower punch - Family Treasures; Ribbon - Local craft store;
Flower Border - Linda's own design; Brads - American Tag Co.; Chalk - Craf-T Products; Pen - Zig Writer, EK Success; Font - Unknown

Tae Kwan Do
State Championship

by Kathleen Linder

SUPPLIES

Lettering Template - Mt. Range, Scrap Pagerz
Cardstock - Bazzill Basics Paper
Fibers - Local fabric store
Eyelets - Making Memories
Pen - Zig Writer, EK Success
Chalk - Craf-T Products
Title font - Kathleen's own handwriting
Font - Unknown

Laser cut - Deluxe Cuts

Adding a Laser die cut, or any other themed shaped paper-piece to a title enhances the title and the page.

We want some SIZZLE, not a bunch of drizzle

by Linda Jones

SUPPLIES Letter Templates - Grade School, Scrap Pagerz and Provo Craft; Cardstock - Bazzill Basics Paper and Renae Lindgren Cardstock, Creative Imaginations; White Pen - Galaxy Marker, American Crafts; Pen - Zig Writer, EK Success; Font - Linda's own handwriting

Die Cuts

Die cut letters and titles are simple to use and impressive on a finished page. They offer the versatility of stencil letters without the hassle of handcutting them out. Die cutting systems come in a variety of sizes and are simple to use. Most scrapbook stores have large Ellison and/or Accu-Cut machines to use. There are also personal die cutting systems, like QuicKutz and Sizzix, which are small and can be transported to crops as well as used at home. You can also purchase pre-cut titles and letters which are available from many different companies.

In this section, we have provided several lettering styles from a few different sources. We have demonstrated how the same letter style can be used for a variety of different themes, and how you can get a perfectly customized look without much work.

Cute
by Judy Martineck

SUPPLIES

Die cut letters - Sonja, QuicKutz
Blue striped paper - Doodlebug Designs
Pink pattern paper - Bryce and Madeline,
    Creative Imaginations
Blue gingham - Daisy D's
Eyelets - American Tag Co.
Cardstock and vellum - Bazzill Basics Paper
Twistel - Making Memories
Denim Pocket - Design by Amber
    Bittenbender
Circle punches - Family Treasures
    and Fiskars
Stitching - As You Wish (Sewing Machine)
Pen - Zig Writer, EK Success
Ribbon - Local craft store
Chalk - Craf-T Products
Pop Dots - All Night Media
Font - Mariah, Microsoft Word

The Age of Innocence
by Laura Fischer

SUPPLIES

Die cut letters - Sonja, QuicKutz
Cardstock and vellum - Bazzill Basics Paper
Bear - Paper Bliss
Heart punch - Family Treasures
Fibers - Creative Imaginations
Brads - Ting-A-Lings, Carolees Creations
Pen - Micron, Sakura
Font - CK Signature

Hint - Laura used a paper trimmer to create the squares, but you could also use a square punch.

In the Garden
by Amber Bittenbender

SUPPLIES

Die cut letters - Khaki, QuicKutz
Background paper - Sonnets by Sharon Soneff, Creative Imaginations
Cardstock - Bazzill Basics Paper
Metal Corners and Frames - Making Memories
Brads - Ting-A-Lings, Carolees Creations
Flower punch - Family Treasures
Hole punch - Fiskars
Box label holder - IKEA
Flowers - Amber's own design
Fonts - Pristina and Times New Roman
Clip art - Printmaster Gold

Hint: To make the letters for GARDEN, punch out flowers, punch a hole in center, then glue them to green cardstock before cutting them.

Love
by Judy Martineck

SUPPLIES

Die cut letters - Sonja, QuicKutz
Background paper - Daisy D's
Tan border paper - Daisy D's
Brads - Ting-A-Lings, Carolees Creations
Raffia - Local craft store
Daisy pattern - Judy's own design
Vellum - Bazzill Basic Paper
Cardstock- Bazzill Basics Paper
Pen - Zig Writer, EK Success
Chalk pencils - Cretacolor, BF Hirm Austria
Chalk - Craf-T Products
Pop Dots - All Night Media
Font - Kristen ITC, Microsoft Word

There's nothing more wonderful than a daughter who brings her father a bouquet of her love. The "hugs and kisses" and "I love you's" from such a sweet and innocent child can be matched by nothing else. It's moments like these we will treasure forever.

Sweet Valentine
by Jennifer Archuleta

SUPPLIES

Die cut letters - Sonja, QuicKutz; Background Paper - The Paper Company;
Bradwear- Creative Imaginations; Black and red brads - Ting-A-Lings, Carolees
Creations; Heart die cut - QuicKutz; Thread - Stitches, Making Memories

Valentines Day 2003
by Mychael Rodriguez

SUPPLIES
Die cut title - Sonja, QuicKutz; Background paper - The Paper Company; Cardstock and vellum - Bazzill Basics Paper;
Heart die cuts - QuicKutz; Brads - Ting-A-Lings, Carolees Creations; Bradwear - Creative Imaginations;
Fibers - Stitches, Making Memories; Paper Piercer - Making Memories; Font - Unknown

Cookies
by Judy Martineck

SUPPLIES
Die cut letters - Star, QuicKutz; Striped paper - k.p. kids & co., Paper Adventures; Cardstock and vellum - Bazzill Basics Paper; Brads - Ting-A-Lings,
Carolees Creations; Fibers - Local craft store; Tag Die Cut - American Tag Co; Rolling Pin die cut - Judy's own design; Micro Beads - Magic Scraps;
Cotton Balls - Local drug store; Chalk - Craf-T Products; Cookie Cutter die cuts - Judy's own design; Font - CK Journaling

A Little Bit of This, A Little Bit of That...

This section barely touches on all the other ways you can create a title. The first group of products to mention, which probably should have had its own section, is titles made with sticker letters. In the past two years, the manufacturers have produced some awesome sticker letters. Some are even embossed and so precisely cut that they appear to be your own art work. Letters now come in many different fonts, styles, sizes and colors and many of these sticker letters are repositionable and easy to work with.

There are many pre-made titles that are very fast and easy to use. These titles are either made with colors appropriate for the theme or made with black lettering on vellum. Other products used to make titles are tags, wood and metal tiles, pebbles, wire, brads, rub-ons, stamps, punch-outs and beads. Lastly, you can make a title with your own design, style and handwriting. Some of the layouts have used two different types of products to create a very distinctive title. Everyone has leftover sticker sheets from which you only used maybe 10 letters. Try making a title mixing and matching, or not matching, with all those leftover sticker letters.

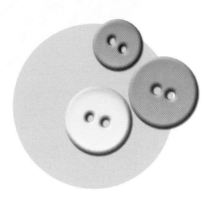

Ian's First Carnival Ride
by Jenny Benge

SUPPLIES

Sticker letters - Shotz, Creative Imaginations,
   Doodlebug Designs and K I Memories
Stamps - Impress Rubber Stamps
Cardstock - Bazzill Basics Paper
Circle punch - Family Treasures
Buttons - Making Memories
Pen - Pigma Micron, Sakura

Lil Scooter Dude
by Jenny Benge

SUPPLIES

Title Stickers - Sonnets by Sharon Soneff, Creative Imaginations,
   Making Memories, and David Walker, Colorbok
Pattern paper - Scrapbook Interiors, Chatterbox
Cardstock - Bazzill Basics Paper
Eyelets - Making Memories
Raffia - Local craft store
Font - CK Fraternity

Travels Border
by Amber Bittenbender

SUPPLIES

Title - Impress-on Bradwear,
   Creative Imaginations
Brads - Ting-A-Lings, Carolees Creations
Pattern papers - Sonnets by Sharon Soneff,
   Creative Imaginations
Cardstock - Bazzill Basics Paper
Eyelets - Creative Impressions
Page Pebbles - Making Memories

Friendship is... Brothers
by Jennifer Archuleta

SUPPLIES

Title - Impress-on Bradwear,
   Creative Imaginations
Font - CK Higgins Handprint
Cardstock and vellum - Bazzill Basics Paper
Tag - Handmade by Jennifer
Frog and Lizard - QuicKutz
Twine - Local craft store

Ashlee signed up for a session of indoor SOCCER in Salmon Creek. She had a blast running, kicking and learning to pass the ball. She blocked goals, made a goal or two and was a good sport about it all. Her teammates all were fun and her coach was impressed with her effort.

MAR 2002

Soccer Star
by Jenny Benge

SUPPLIES

Title Sticker letters - Sonnets by Sharon Soneff, Creative Imaginations
Letter Eyelets - Making Memories
Star Eyelets - Making Memories
Cardstock - Bazzill Basics Paper
Fibers - Local craft store
Font - 2Peas Flea Market Blocks and P22 Garmouche by Impress Rubber Stamps
Date Stamp - Office supply store
Pen - Zig Writer, EK Success

Hint:
Jenny had a great idea for her slide frame. She took two frames and cut the top off one and the bottom off the other one. Then put them back together to make one long frame.

This Garden...
by Jenny Benge

SUPPLIES

Title stamps - Impress Rubber Stamps, Bunch of Fun and PSX
Title - Jenny's handwriting
Paper - Mustard Moon
Buttons - Dress It Up
Slide Frame - Impress Rubber Stamps
Fibers - Adornaments, EK Success
Watercan Charm - Blue Moon Beads
Stamps - Impress Rubber Stamps, Bunch of Fun & PSX
Ink - SU! Close to Cocoa
Garden Design - Jenny Benge
Pens - Brown and Black Zig Writer, EK Success
Shape Clips - Unknown

this garden HAS GOT TO GO!

With fall weather fast approaching, the kids enjoyed one last time in the garden, tearing it out and tossing everything in the woods.
October 2002

Happy Birthday

by Gretchen Schmidt

SUPPLIES

Title and accents - Klip-Its, Kopp Design
Plum plaid and solid paper - Kopp Design
Oatmeal cardstock - Making Memories
Pen - Zig Millennium, EK Success

Fun in the Sun
by Linda Jones

SUPPLIES

Sticker letters - SEI
Paper - SEI
Border stickers - SEI
Tags - DMD Industries
Fibers - Adornaments, EK Success
Eyelets - American Tag Co.
Stitching - Done with sewing machine
Pen - Zig Writer, EK Success

Shoes on all by myself
by Jenny Benge

SUPPLIES

Title Sticker - Doodlebug Designs; Title Stamps - Impress Rubber Stamps;
Cardstock - Bazzill Basics Paper; Mirrored Star - Impress Rubber Stamps;
Metal circle tags - American Tag Co.; Buttons - Dress it Up; Star eyelets, star
charms and snaps - Making Memories; Star brads - Creative Imaginations;
Pen - Zig Writer, EK Success; Date stamp - Office supply store

Gone Fishing
by Judy Martineck

SUPPLIES

Title Cutouts - Rebecca Sower Fresh Cuts,
  EK Success
Cardstock, vellum and double-sided
  handmade paper - Bazzill Basics Paper
Netting - Stop-n-Crop
Chalk - Craf-T Products
Scott's Trophy font - Judy's own handwriting
Font - CK Journaling

Meet me
by the Seashore

by Judy Martineck

SUPPLIES

Title and phrase - Quick Quotes
Background paper - Glad Tidings
Cardstock and vellum - Bazzill Basics Paper
Shell stickers - Stickopotamus, EK Success
Font - Kristin ITC

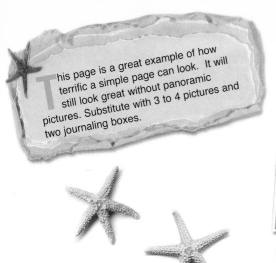

This page is a great example of how terrific a simple page can look. It will still look great without panoramic pictures. Substitute with 3 to 4 pictures and two journaling boxes.

Surfer Boys

by Tara Stevenson

SUPPLIES

Title Font - Tara's design; Background paper - NRN Designs; Flower border - NRN Designs; Cardstock and vellum - Bazzill Basics Paper; Surfboard die cut - Tara's design; Pen - Zig Writer; Font - Unknown

First Communion
by Nidia Peralta

SUPPLIES

Title - Nidia's own handwriting; Background vellum - unknown; Gold paper - NRN Designs; Bow - Anna Griffin; Ribbon - Local craft store; Verse sticker - Printworks; Banner template - C-Thru Ruler Company; Flower punch - Marvy Uchida; Petal punch - Punch Bunch; Hole punch - Fiskars; Wire - Westrim Crafts; Gold pen - Galaxy marker, American Crafts; Chalk - Craf-T Products

Beach Vacation
by Linda Jones

SUPPLIES

Tag title - Lil' Davis Designs; Pattern paper - Daisy D's; Cardstock and vellum - Bazzill Basics Paper; Twine - Local craft store; Font - Mom's Typewriter

Spring Blossoms
by Linda Jones

SUPPLIES

Title Font - Linda's own handwriting
Tag - Linda's own design
Background paper - Deja Views
Cardstock - Bazzill Basics Paper
Flower and leaf punch - Family Treasures
Flower pot punch - Emaginations
Brads - American Tag Co.
Chalk - Craf-T Products
Raffia - Local craft store
Pen - Zig Writer, EK Success
Font - Boys R Gross

This page can easily be altered to suit your needs - just take a picture of your girls dressed up nice, no matter what time of the year.

Planting Bee Bait
by Linda Jones

SUPPLIES

Title font - Linda's own handwriting; Plaid paper - Cut-it-Up; Cardstock and vellum - Bazzill Basics Paper; Brads - American Tag Co.;
Flower and bee cutouts - Rebecca Sower Fresh Tags, EK Success

Bike ridin'
by Jenny Benge

SUPPLIES

Title - Jenny's own handwriting
Large buttons - Making Memories
Fibers - On the Fringe
Key tag - Avery
Punch - Punch Bunch
Mini buttons - Dress It Up
Brown tag - Jenny's design
Brads - American Tag Co.
Pattern paper - Lasting Impressions
White tags - Unknown
Font - Jenny's handwriting

daughter
by Jenny Benge

SUPPLIES

Title font and journaling - Liorah BT

Pocket journaling - Downloaded
    from Two Peas

Pattern paper - KI Memories

Cardstock & vellum -
    Bazzill Basics Paper

Fibers - On the Fringe

Heart eyelets - Making Memories

Stitching - Singer sewing machine

Discover
by Linda Jones

SUPPLIES

Title - Sonnets Wire Expressions,
    Creative Imaginations
Pattern paper - Sonnets by Sharon Soneff,
    Creative Imaginations
Fibers - Unknown
Heart eyelets - Unknown
Cardstock & vellum - Bazzill Basic Paper
Tag - Linda's design
Font - Linda's handwriting

Simple Pleasures
of Summer
by Linda Jones

SUPPLIES

Title Font - Linda's handwriting
Background paper - Sonnets by Sharon Soneff,
    Creative Imaginations
Blue border paper - Sharon Soneff,
    Creative Imaginations
Cardstock - Bazzil Basics Paper
Flower pattern - Linda's Pattern
Wire - Westrim Crafts
Pen - Zig Writer, EK Success
Ribbon - Local Craft Store
Chalk - Craft-T Products

On a

warm

spring day,

nothin'

tastes

yummier

than

OTTER POPS

Zachary - 3 years
Cameron - 14 mos.

Otter Pops
by Jennifer Archuleta

SUPPLIES:

Title fonts - CK Journaling, CK Warm Breeze, CK
    Butterfly, CK Kiddo, CK Long and Lanky
Letter beads - Westrim Crafts
Cardstock and vellum - Bazzill Basics Paper
Pattern paper - Unknown
Fibers - Adornaments, EK Success
Brad - Ting-A-Lings, Carolees Creations
Vellum tag - Making Memories

Jennifer cut strips of cardstock
at slightly different angles and
mounted them behind the
brochure to draw attention. She
cut scenic photos into one inch
squares and put them under her
journaling. She used two eyelets
to hold the journaling so that you
could lift the vellum to better see
the photos. She tore and rolled
the title to age it. She chalked it
first with green, then with black to
darken the edges and attached
the title with wire.

Auntie's 50th Birthday Getaway

by Jennifer Archuleta

SUPPLIES:

Letters - Jennifer's own design and Simply Stated, Making Memories;
Cardstock and vellum - Bazzill Basics Paper; Eyelets - Making Memories;
Fibers - Creative Imaginations; Word stickers - Bo Bunny Press;
Alphabet tiles - Savvy Tiles, Creative Imaginations; Metal Frame - Making Memories;
Chalk – Craf-T Products; Brad – American Tag Co; Font – CK Script

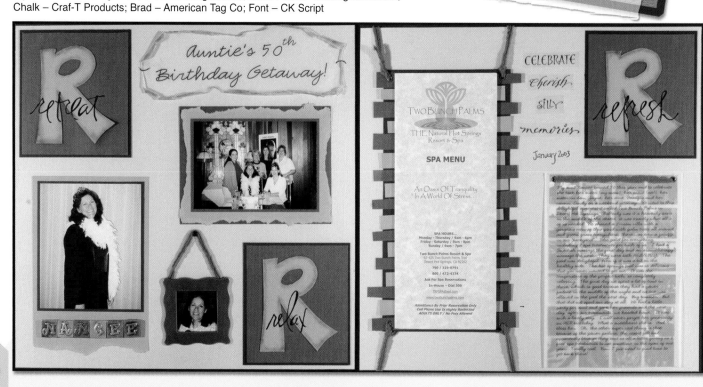

Disney
by Judy Martineck

SUPPLIES

Title Fonts - Curlz, Dayco Ltd
Balloon and tag die cuts - Paper Wizard
Cardstock - Bazzill Basics Paper
Pattern paper - Doodlebug Designs
Fibers - Stitches, Making Memories
Pens - Zig Writer and Zig Scroll Brush,
    EK Success
Eyelet - American Tag
Font on tag - CK Stenography
Chalk - Craf-T Products

Paradise Found
by Amber Bittenbender

SUPPLIES

Title - Simply Stated, Making Memories
Cardstock and vellum - Bazzill Basics Paper
Shells - Magic Scraps
Chalk - Craf-T Products

Pick of the Patch
by Amber Bittenbender
SUPPLIES   Title font - Handwritten, traced from CK Inky; Pattern paper - Bo Bunny Press;
Cardstock and vellum - Bazzill Basic Paper; Wire - Westrim Crafts; Pumpkins - Oval punches, Family Treasures; Leaf - Family
Treasures; Chalk - Craf-T Products; Pen - Zig Writer, EK Success

Look Who's Three
by Amber Bittenbender

SUPPLIES

Title die cuts - Sizzix and Ignacio
Candles - Sizzix
Pattern papers - Doodlebug Designs
Cardstock - Bazzill Basics Paper
Pens - Zig Writers, EK Success,
    and white gel pen by Mary Uchica

Various Artists

This section of the book has been laid out to introduce a few of our artistic designers so that you can become acquainted with each designer's unique style and talent.

Jenny Benge

I live in SW Washington State with my husband and our three children: Ashlee, Amanda and Ian - who, of course, are the main subjects of my work. I have been scrapping for 5-years and in addition to working on the Scrapbook Sampler series, I design for Embelleez, I am a Design Team member at Scrapjazz.com and teach at my favorite (not-so-local) scrapbook store, Art House in Portland, Oregon.

I've been published in Creating Keepsakes, Simple Scrapbooks, PaperKuts, Ivy Cottage Creations, Scrapbooks Etc., Memory Makers and was a contributor to "The Complete Idiot's Guide to Scrapbooking."

When I'm not scrapbooking or thinking about it, I like to do yard work, decorate our home, shop and sometimes I even sew and bake cookies!

Jenny

Love You

SUPPLIES

Tags - Designed by Jenny; Extreme Eyelets - Creative Imaginations; Fibers - On the Surface; Button - Dress It Up; Square Punch - Family Treasures; Pen - Pigma Micron, Sakura; Chalk - Craf-T Products; Font - Bean Sprout; Date stamp - Office Depot; Jenny's inspiration came from a Becky Higgins sketch.

Big Boy Bike

SUPPLIES

Tags - American Tag Co.
Pattern paper - Pebbles, Inc
Sticker letters - Doodlebug
    Design Inc.
Frame, Twistel & Date stamp -
    Making Memories
Brads - Karen Foster and
    Caroles Creations
Bradwear -
    Creative Imaginations
Swirl clip - Target
Pen - Pigma Micron, Sakura
Font - Inkster downloaded
    from the Internet
Letter Stamps - Unknown

I Will Push You

SUPPLIES

Tag - Avery
Stickers - Sonnets, Creative Imaginations; Ribbon - May Arts; Ink - Staz On; Pen - Zig Writer, EK Success

As I looked at several of Jenny's great pages, I've realized that one of her talents for making her layouts simple, yet special, is her color scheme. In most of her layouts, she carefully chooses 2 to 3 colors out of the photographs. Then she picks matching colored cardstock, some pattern paper, and various embellishments.

Watermelon

SUPPLIES

Tag - Designed by Jenny
Brads - American Tag Co.
Twistel - Making Memories
Sticker letters - Doodlebug Design Inc.
    and Sonnets, Creative Imaginations
Buttons - Dress It Up and Making Memories
Pattern paper - Pebbles, Inc.
Cardstock - Monochromatics, Bazzill Basic Paper
Pen - Zig Writer, EK Success

Popsicle Time

SUPPLIES

Tag and Popsicle - Designed by Jenny
Sticker letters - Sue Dreamer, Colorbok
Pattern paper - unknown
DMC floss - Local craft store
Twistel - Making Memories
Eyelets - Doodlebug Design Inc.
Pen - Zig Writer, EK Success

Birthday Boy Tags

SUPPLIES

Tag template - Coluzzle; Pattern paper - Making Memories;
Sticker letters - David Walker, Creative Imaginations;
Eyelets - Doodlebug Design Inc. and Dritz; Twistel - Making
Memories; Fibers - DMD Industries; Chalk - Craf-T Products;
Pen - Zig Writer, EK Success

Blacky

SUPPLIES

Tags - American Tag Co.
Sticker Letters - Doodlebug Design Inc.
Maruyama - Magenta
Hearts - Designed by Jenny
Stamps - Personal Stamp Exchange
Ribbon - May Arts
Heart Brad - Carolees Creations
Heart Eyelet - Making Memories
Buttons - Dress It Up
Dotlets - Doodlebug Design Inc.
Ink - Paintbox
Pen - Pigma Micron, Sakura and Scroll & Brush, EK Success

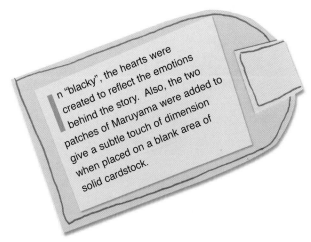

n "blacky", the hearts were created to reflect the emotions behind the story. Also, the two patches of Maruyama were added to give a subtle touch of dimension when placed on a blank area of solid cardstock.

Hot Summer Time Tags

SUPPLIES

Tag template - Coluzzle, Provo Craft; Sticker letters - Paper Fever
Brads - Making Memories; Buttons - Magic Scraps
Fiber - Club Scrap; Glass beads - Visual Image Printery
Pens - Zig Writer, EK Success
and Pigma Micron, Sakura

Summer Hairdo
SUPPLIES

Square punch for tag effect - Punch Bunch
Pattern paper - Pebbles, Inc
Two-toned cardstock - Paper Adventures
Sticker letters - Penny Black and Doodlebug Design Inc.
Brads - Karen Foster
Flower punch - Punch Bunch
Raffia - Sample House
Pen - Zig Writer, EK Success

Silly

SUPPLIES

Circles for the tag "look" - Creative Memories
Word titles - Magnetic Poetry
Poetry dog tag - Chronicle Books
Metal letters - Making Memories
Stamps - Bunch of Fun
Heart - Heidi Grace
Ribbon - Offray
Ink - Staz On
Date stamp - Local office supply store

Inspirations can sometimes come when least expected. Jenny was inspired to do this page while looking at a Target store advertisement.

Spring at G-Ma and G-Pa

SUPPLIES: Tags - Designed by Jenny; Cardstock - Monochromatics, Bazzill Basics Paper; Ink - Stampin' Up; Stamps - Impress Rubber Stamps, Bunch of Fun & Personal Stamp Exchange; Extreme Eyelets - Creative Imaginations; Washers - Lowes; Metal flower brads - Making Memories; Metallic Rub-On - Craf-T Products; Fibers - On the Surface, On the Fringe and Jest Charming; Date stamp - Local office supply store; Stitching - By Jenny

Ian

SUPPLIES

Tag - Designed by Jenny
Fibers - Adornments, EK Success
Stamps - Hero Arts, Bunch
    of Fun and Personal Stamp Exchange
Ink - Paintbox (blue) and Versamark (brown)
Embossing Powder - All Night Media
Brads and eyelet - American Tag Co.
Date stamp - Local office supply store
Pen - Zig Writer and Scroll & Brush, EK Success

Beary Sweet

SUPPLIES

Tags - American Tag Co.
Pattern vellum - Chatterbox
Sticker letters - Sue Dreamer,
    Colorbok and Doodlebug Design Inc,
    Circle letters were slightly sanded.
Bears - Basic Bear
Fibers - On the Fringe
Brads - American Tag Co.
Date stamp - Making Memories
Metallic rub-on and chalk - Craf-T Products
Pen - Pigma Micron, Sakura

December 2002

Fall '03 Tag

SUPPLIES

Tag template - Coluzzle, Provo Craft
Rose leaf and square punch - The Punch Bunch
Eyelet - American Tag Co.
Fibers - On the Surface
Stamps - Postmodern Design
Ink - Marvy Uchida
Metallic Rub-On - Craf-T Products
Pen - Zig Millennium, EK Success

I Can Still Remember…

SUPPLIES: Tag - American Tag Co.; Sticker letters - Sonnets, Creative Imaginations; Metal letters - Making Memories; Brads - American Tag Co.; Ribbon - Local craft store; Letter stamps - Bunch of Fun; Ink - Marvy Uchida; Metallic Rub-On - Craf-T Products; Staples and date stamp - Local office supply store; Pen - Pigma Micron, Sakura; Font - Flea Market, downloaded from twopeasinabucket.com

10 Reasons to Love Amanda

SUPPLIES

Tags - Avery; Sticker letters - David Walker, Creative Imaginations; Vellum - Golden Oak; Eyelets - Eyelet Doctor; Hearts - Cut down from a McGill flower punch; Photo corners - Canson; Chalk - Craf-T Products; Pen - Pigma Micron, Sakura; Font - CK Penman

To make the tags unique and match the page, the white part of the tags were unevenly chalked with red. The dark and light colors give it character and you don't have to worry about the tags coming out the same color. The ties on the tags were thin strips of white paper carefully placed through the eyelets and tied in a knot.

Rose Tag

SUPPLIES

Tag - Designed by Jenny
Corrugated paper - DMD
    Industries
Rose - Designed by Jenny
Ribbon - Offray
Ink - Staz On

The Conchos on top of the ribbon are a great way to hold down both the ribbon and the fibers. They also create a unique look when used to accent the hole at the top of a tag.

All of God's grace in one sweet face

SUPPLIES

Tag template - Coluzzle, Provo Craft
Monochromatic cardstock and
    handmade paper - Bazzill Basics Paper
Picture corners - Canson
Fibers - Fibers by the Yard and
    from a local fabric store
Conchos - Scrapworks
Heart charm - Westrim Crafts
Font - Valentina JF, downloaded from the Internet

Kindergarten Graduate

SUPPLIES

Tags - Avery and Impress Rubber Stamps
Pattern paper - Lasting Impressions
Cutouts - Paper Fever
Brads - Karen Foster
Heart eyelets - unknown
Ribbon - May Arts
Stamps - Bunch of Fun and Impress Rubber Stamps
Ink - SU!
Date stamp - Local office supply store

Linda Porter Jones

Hi! My name is Linda Porter Jones, and I'm addicted to Scrapping! I live in Long Beach, CA with my husband of 22 years, Gary, and our six children. Needless to say, with that many kids I NEVER run out of photo ops or layouts to create!

I started scrapping 6 years ago (the "right way"), though I kept photo albums and scrapbooks all through my teen years. What started as a plan to organize and preserve our family photos, quickly became an obsession and creative outlet. I've given up trying to stay "caught up'" and instead enjoy the fun and creativity of creating scrapbook pages that please me and my family.

I've been lucky to teach at Scrapbook Depot for the last 4 years. In addition to the Scrapbook Sampler series, I've had my work published in Creating Keepsakes, PaperKuts, Ivy Cottage Creations and Pinecone Press books. I'm on a few scrapbooking design teams and I also design work for CROPYcats, 2000 Keepsakes, and Memories of the Rabbit.

Many thanks to Judy, the Scrapbook Depot staff and all my class scrappers for their support and friendship.
HAPPY SCRAPPING!!

Linda

Graduation Memories 2003

SUPPLIES

Tag - Designed by Linda; Graduation cap, scroll and rolled diploma - Designed by Linda; Tassel - Wrights Trim; Pattern paper - Deja Views; Cardstock and vellum - Bazzill Basics Paper; Eyelets and brads - American Tag Co.; Templates - Calligraphy, Scrap Pagerz; Chalk - Craf-T Products; Pen - Zig Writer, EK Success; Font - Script, MS Word

Our Summer Vacation

SUPPLIES

Tags - DMD Industries
Pattern paper - 7 Gypsies
Eyelets, rivets and brads - American Tag Co.
Buttons and fabric ribbon - Local craft store
Splatter Net - Jest Charming Embellishments
Chain - Making Memories
Metallic Rub-Ons and chalk - Craf-T Products

Back to School

SUPPLIES

Tag - DMD Industries
Pattern papers - Sweetwater and Deja Views
Cardstock - Bazzill Basics Paper
Rivets and brads - American Tag Co.
Ribbon - Wrights Trim
Jute cording - Local Craft store
Chalk - Craf-T Products
Font - Lettera 32, downloaded from the Internet

Back to School Tag

SUPPLIES

Tags - DMD
Stickers - Debbie Mumm, Creative Imaginations
Pattern paper - Sweetwater and Deja Views
Fabric - Local craft store
Apple - Jolee's, EK Success
Pen - Zig Writer, EK Success

God Bless the USA

SUPPLIES

Tags - Designed by Linda
Pattern paper - Scrap-Ease, Daisy D's
   and Lasting Impressions
Vellum - Bazzill Basics Paper
Letter stencil - Party, Scrap Pagerz
Star punches - Emaginations
Gold circle clip - Making Memories
Brads - American Tag Co.
Fabric - Local craft store
Ink - ColorBox, Clearsnap
Pen - Zig Writer, EK Success
Font - CB Wednesday

Our 4th of July celebrations this year included a block party and bike parade. The girls spent the morning decorating their bikes with bows, flags, and streamers. The effect was quite patriotic, and the bike parade was a huge success!

For a cute center on the stars, cut a thin strip of cardstock and tie it into a knot. Change the color of the plain white tags by chalking them to match your layout. Try inking the edges of the border strips, journaling boxes and shapes for a rustic look. Just drag the edges of the item carefully through the ink-box, set aside to dry before adhering to the layout.

Sweet Land of Liberty

SUPPLIES

Tag - Designed by Linda; Pattern Paper - Lasting Impressions; Eyelets - American Tag Co.; Star punches - Emaginations; Twine - Local craft store; White gel pen - Marvy Uchida; Paper piecing pattern - by Donna Garza

Hittin' the Trail
SUPPLIES

Tag - Designed by Linda, inspired by Stephanie Rarick; Pattern paper - 7 Gypsies; Paper piecing pattern - CROPYcats;
Lettering template - Watermelon, Scrap Pagerz; Star brads and Extreme Eyelets - Creative Imaginations;
Nailheads - American Tag Co.; Burlap, fabric and twine - Local craft store; Ink - ColorBox, Clearsnap;
Chalk - Craf-T Products; Pen - Zig Writer, EK Success; Font - Nashville and Times, downloaded from the Internet

Here Linda has created a lively, fun page that would also look great with boy photos. The simplicity is not only striking, but it's a fast and easy page to put together.

Be My Pal
SUPPLIES

Tags - DMD Industries
Pattern paper - Picture Perfect
Brads and buttons - Embelleez
Twine - Local craft store
Chalk - Craf-T Products
Pen - Zig Writer, EK Success
Font - Times New Roman, MS Word
Tag Letters - Linda's hand writing

You Hold the Key to my Heart

SUPPLIES

Tags - Designed by Linda; Key tag - CROPYcats; Lettering template - Scrap Pagerz; Heart punch - Emaginations; Brads - American Tag Co.; Fibers - Unknown; Wire, letter beads, gems and glass beads - Westrim Crafts; Title font - Times New Roman, MS Word

Halloween Fun

SUPPLIES

Tags - Designed by Linda; Lettering template - Mountain Range, Scrap Pagerz; Eyelets - American Tag Co.; Star punch – Emaginations; Brads - American Crafts; Twine - Local craft store; Chalk - Craf-T Products; Pens - Zig Writer, EK Success and White gel pen, Marvy Uchida; Paper piecing pattern - By Donna Garza

How to be Jenni...

- Be a risk taker
- Enjoy trying new things
- Amaze Mom with your beauty and style
- Like boys (!!!)
- Be confident in your talents and abilities
- Know how to "twist" Dad around your little finger
- Speak your mind when necessary
- Be charming and loving

Here Linda shows us how to make a great page for a teenager. I really think this is important because they change so much in those years of searching for their own identity and independence. Instead of trying to write a couple of paragraphs of heartfelt journaling, Linda jotted down a list instead. You could list attributes, their favorite things or funny things they say or do.

How to be Jenni...
SUPPLIES

Tags - Designed by Jenny; Pattern paper and stickers - Pamela Woods, Creative Imaginations; Cardstock, double-sided handmade paper and handmade paper - Bazzill Basics Paper; Rivets - Scrapbook Interiors, Chatterbox; Metal numbers - Making Memories; Cotton twine - Local craft store; Chalk and Metallic Rub-Ons - Craf-T Products; Font - Amalie Script

Cami
SUPPLIES

Tags template - Deluxe Cuts
Pattern paper and stickers -
    Pamela Woods, Creative Imaginations
Cardstock - Monochromatics,
    Bazzill Basics Paper
Metallic letters - Embellez
Cotton twine - Local craft store
Sticks - Found on a nature hike
Pen - Zig Writer, EK Success

April · 03

On a trip to Santa Ana creek, Cami was thrilled to discover large patches of wild-flowers growing along the water's edge

Judy Martineck

Hi, my name is Judy Martineck and I, too, am addicted to scrapbooking and work! I have the privilege to do both as much as I want, since I am a single parent of two older teenagers.

I started scrapbooking twelve years ago as a Creative Memories consultant. My plan was just to organize my photos and put them into albums so my kids would remember their childhood. In my early 20's, I took every art class there was, not knowing that twenty years later I would be using it to design-paint furniture, murals on walls, and later for designing scrapbook pages and books. Also in my mid 20's, I took business and accounting classes, again not knowing I would own my own business later. In between, I had four or five other careers from sales to nursing, and here I am now.

I have no published credits - the only recognition I've received for my layouts is from my children and my customers. And I thank them so much for all of their positive support and comments.

Judy

Angels of mine
SUPPLIES

Tags - Paper Bliss, Westrim Crafts; Background paper - Paper Bliss, Westrim Crafts; Vellum - Bazzill Basics Paper; Buttons and flowers - Paper Bliss Accent Kit, Westrim Crafts; Fibers - Adornaments, EK Success; Sticker Letters - David Walker, Creative Imaginations; Letter stamps - Personal Stamp Exchange; Chalk - Craf-T Products; Pen - Zig Writer, EK Success; Font - Comic Sans

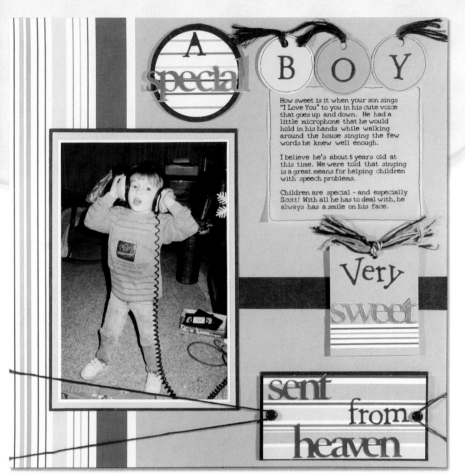

How sweet is it when your son sings "I Love You" to you in his cute voice that goes up and down. He had a little microphone that he would hold in his hands while walking around the house singing the few words he knew well enough.

I believe he's about 5 years old at this time. We were told that singing is a great means for helping children with speech problems.

Children are special – and especially Scott! With all he has to deal with, he always has a smile on his face.

Very sweet

sent from heaven

A Special Boy

SUPPLIES

All tags - SEI cutouts
Pattern paper - SEI
Metal words - Making Memories
Letters - Paige Mini's, QuicKutz
Fibers - Stitches, Making Memories
Vellum - Bazzill Basics Paper
Brads - Carolees Creations
Double-sided handmade paper -
    Bazzill Basics Paper
Pen - Zig Writer, EK Success
Font - PC Inky

Why me?

SUPPLIES

Tags - Designed by Judy
Pattern paper and fibers - Scrapbook Sally
Vellum - Bazzill Basics Paper
Brads - Bradlets, Provo Craft
Hearts - Tokens, Doodlebug Design Inc.
Metal letters - Making Memories
Chalk - Craf-T Products
Pen - Zig Writer, EK Success
Fonts - CK Script, CK Cute,
    CK Teacher's Pet, CK Easygoing,
    CK Daydream; CK Typeset

Prom Night

SUPPLIES

Tuxedo Tag - Designed by Judy
Bow tie - Designed by Judy
Prom Night title - Griff's Shortcuts
Silver sparkle paper - Making Memories
Star vellum - Printworks
Black metallic paper and vellum -
    Bazzill Basics Paper
Vellum quote - Quick Quotes
Brads - American Tag Co.
Music notes and stars - Meri Meri
Font - CK Journaling

This layout could be converted to any special occasion. The New Years tag would be a great substitute for the Prom Night. New Year SUPPLIES: Tag - Cut a circle the size you would like out of Sparkle paper (Making Memories) and a star out of white cardstock. Write your title and then glue some Shaved Ice (Magic Scraps) on the star. Mat the circle and star with black paper (shiny or flat) and cut the center strip 1" wide. Punch out several silver stars or use stickers to place on the strip. Punch out a hole and add a festive silver ribbon.

Sarah

SUPPLIES
Tag - DMD Inc.; Alphabet buttons and zipper - Junkitz; Cardstock - Monochromatics, Bazzill Basics Paper; Maruyama - Magenta; Vellum - Bazzill Basics Paper; Thread - Local Craft Store; Chalk - Chalklets, EK Success; Pop Dots - All Night Media; Font - Ariel and CK Inky.

Thrilled

SUPPLIES

Tag - Designed by Judy
Background paper - SEI
Handmade paper - Bazzill Basics Paper
Sticker letters - Sassy, Sticker Studio
Large letters - Venus, QuicKutz
Fibers - Scrapbook Sally
Pen - Zig Writer, EK Success
Chalk - Chalklets, EK Success
Font - CK Journaling

Carnival Elation Cabo San Lucas Mexico

Thrilled
Excited
Real
Cool
'98
Awesome

We were waiting for the boat taxi to come and pick us up and take us back to the ship. Sarah and Kendall had fun shopping at the flee market. I had fun buying a glass knife. However, I thought it was really cool that this man wanted to take my picture with his iguana on my head. It was kinda big and heavy and I really didn't want him to move.

This layout could probably work for just about any activity a boy does – whether fishing or sports!

The Love of Camping

1991

It's not just looking at the fluffy white clouds or the tall ominous trees.

It's also not the sounds of the brooks or the songs of the birds or even the quietness surrounding us.

And let's not forget to mention the smells that are so clean and natural.

My Love for Camping is definitely about all the above but is more about being with my children and sharing this peaceful time and space with them.

Our favorite Camping Place
Mammoth

Make your own small tag for the date – it's easy and adds a fun embellishment to the page!

The Love of Camping

SUPPLIES

Aged tag - 7 Gypsies
Small tag - Designed by Judy
Cardstock - Monochromatics,
    Bazzill Basics Paper
Maruyama - Magenta
Vellum - Bazzill Basics Paper
Sticker letters - David Walker,
    Creative Imaginations
Page pebbles - Making Memories
Mosaic tiles - Magic Scraps
Stamps - Personal Stamp Exchange
Chalk and Metallic Rub-On - Craf-T Products
Font - PK Inky Type

Happy Halloween

SUPPLIES

Tags - QuicKutz
Vellum - Doodlebug Design Inc.
Vellum titles - Quotables, Kopp Designs
Cardstock - Monochromatics, Bazzill
    Basics Paper
Pen - Zig Writer, EK Success and Gel
    Excel, Marvy Uchida
Font - PK Inky Type

To make the Christmas Tree page and to really over-emphasize the tree, I scanned a tree photo, enlarged it to be printed on a $8\frac{1}{2}$ x 11 light weight vellum. Every printer is different, so you might want to buy a few sheets of vellum in case of an error. The light weight vellum didn't smear as much as the heavier weight on my printer. However, you have to hold the side of the light weight vellum as it comes out of the printer to prevent it from curling up. If you don't have a scanner, there are several Christmas papers that could take the place of the vellum.

If you have a particular word in your title you want to emphasize, try using a different font, color, sticker letters, or die cut letters mounted on papers and popped up. The word "Tree" in the title was created different from the rest in this design.

A Christmas Tree Story

SUPPLIES

Tag - Designed by Judy
Gold handmade paper - The Paper Company
Maroon handmade paper - The Lacey
    Paper Company
Green handmade paper - Artistic Scrapper
Cardstock and vellum - Bazzill Basics Paper
Gold clips - Making Memories
Metallic Rub-On - Craf-T Products
Fonts - CK Broadpen, CK Fortune, and
    CK Man's Print

Wish List Tag

SUPPLIES

Tag - Designed by Judy; Wish list tags - Nameplate, QuicKutz;
Mini tags - Designed by Judy; Reindeer die cut - Accu Cut;
Pattern paper - Debbie Mumm, Creative Imaginations;
Metallic and sparkle paper - Making Memories;
Presents - Jolee's by You, EK Success;
Fibers - Fibers & Yarns & Threads, Oh My! Rubba Dub Dub;
Fabric ribbon - Local craft store; DMC floss - Local craft store;
Metallic Rub-On and Chalk - Craf-T Products;
Letter stamps - Celtic, Personal Stamp Exchange;
Pen - Zig Writer, EK Success and Gel Excel, Marvy Uchida;
Fonts - CK Typewriter; Eyes - Westrim Crafts

Trick or Treat Tag

SUPPLIES

Tag - Designed by Judy
Spider die cut - Accu Cut
Typewriter keys - Creative Imaginations
Letters - Paige Mini's, QuicKutz
Cardstock - Monochromatics,
   Bazzill Basics Paper
Splatter net - Jest Charming Embellishments
Googly eyes Westrim Crafts
Fibers - Creative Imaginations
Cording - Local craft store
DMC floss - Local craft store

Joy Tag

SUPPLIES

Tags - Designed by Judy
Letters - Designed by Judy
Pattern paper - Anna Griffin
Fibers - Creative Imaginations
DMC floss - Local craft store
Metallic Rub-On - Craf-T Products
Pen - Zig Writer, EK Success
Note: This tag was inspired by a tag made
   by Stephanie Rarick.

81

Jennifer Lynn Archuleta

Hi! My name is Jennifer Lynn Archuleta. I am 30 years old, born and raised in Long Beach, California. I have been married for 7½ years to my wonderful husband, Matt, and have two boys: Zachary, who is 3½ and Cameron, who is 1½.

I started scrapbooking about 9 years ago after attending a Creative Memories party at a friend's house. I fell in love with the concept of making the "photos and albums" more enjoyable to look at and knowing that it all came from the heart and creativity. I have been working part-time at my local store, Scrapbook Depot, for 6 months and it is so exciting to be right there as new products come out. This hobby brings me so much joy knowing that future generations will be able to enjoy it as much as I do.

Jennifer

How Do You Measure Your Love

SUPPLIES

Tag - Tag Template, Deluxe Cuts
Pattern paper - 7 Gypsies
Dream - Wordz, Creative Imaginations
Button - Dress it Up
Fiber - Magic Scraps
Ink - Ancient Page
Hint - Jennifer sanded the edge of the black and white picture and then chalked it to give it an aged look.

A note by Jennifer

Initially this page was hard for me to start. Thinking that by having black and white pictures for Easter, I wouldn't be able to create much. I continually pushed it aside and then I found the KI Memories paper and it all clicked in my head. I had a lot of pictures and didn't want to leave any out, so I made a little photo book from cardstock. I enclosed it in the torn envelope at the top of the page in the right hand corner. To make the envelope I took a piece of 12x12 paper and placed the photo book in the center of the paper. I then tore the paper to make four torn triangles to cover the book. Then I attached the buttons and string with pop dots. I looped the string around the buttons and pop dots to keep it closed.

Easter

SUPPLIES Tags - Designed by Jennifer; Metal tags - Making Memories; Pattern papers and circle tag words - KI Memories; Sticker letters - David Walker, Colorbok; Typewriter keys - Creative Imaginations; Heart frames - Scrapworks; Eyelet words - Making Memories; Easter eggs and jellybeans - Jolee's by You, EK Success; Buttons - Monochromatic, Junkitz; Fibers - Adornaments, EK Success; DMC floss and ribbon - Local craft store; Date stamp - Making Memories; Pop dots - All Night Media; Pen - Zig Writer, EK Success; Font - CK Footnote

My Sweetheart
by Jennifer Archuleta
Designed by Amber Bittenbender

SUPPLIES

Tag punches - Emaginations;Sticker letters - Doodlebug Design Inc.
Heart brads - Bradlets, Provo Craft; Eyelets - Creative Impressions
DMC floss - Local craft store; Fonts - CK Handprint, CK Fancy,
CK Calligraphy, CK Long and Lanky, CK Diva, CK Script, CK Kiddo,
CK Groovy, DJ Crayon

My Sweetheart (Pink)
by Amber Bittenbender

SUPPLIES

Sticker letters - Teri Martin, Creative Imaginations
Heart brads - Scrap Arts
All other supplies are the same.

Princess Party

SUPPLIES

Tag die cuts - Gift tag circle #2, Accu Cut
Pattern paper and sticker letters - Doodlebug Design Inc.
Metallic paper - Making Memories
Vellum - Hot off the Press
Tiara and wand - Deluxe Cuts
Brads - American Tag Co.
Hole punch - Fiskars
Tiny silver cording - Printworks
Font - CK Diva

Easter Morning
SUPPLIES

Tag - Designed by Jennifer
Pattern paper - San Lori
Vellum - Hot of the Press
Sticker letters - Mrs. Grossman's
Envelope - Deluxe Cuts
Buttons - Dress it Up
Fibers - Creative Imaginations
DMC floss - Local craft store
Pen - Zig Writer, EK Success
"Glue dots" - Glue Dots International
Font - Jennifer's handwriting

A Day at the Park
SUPPLIES

Tag - Designed by Jennifer
Metal tag letters - Making Memories
Cardstock - Monochromatics,
   Bazzill Basics Paper
Vellum - Hot off the Press
Maruyama and charm - Magenta
Primary tiles and fibers - Creative Imaginations
Pewter piece - Paragona Art Emboss
Metal alphabet stamps - Harbor Freight
Watch face - Jest Charming Embellishments
Flower brads - Scrap Arts
Wire - Westrim Crafts
Date stamp – Making Memories
Chalk - Craf-T Products
Font - CK Artisan

A Day at the Park Tag
SUPPLIES

Tag - Designed by Jennifer
Cloud and grass die cut - Accu Cut
Park letters - Primary Tiles, Creative Imaginations
Flower stickers - Stickopotamus
Button and Twistel - Making Memories
Paper raffia - American Tag Co.
DMC floss - Local fabric store
"Glue dots" - Glue Dots International
Chalk - Craf-T Products
Pen - Zig Writer, EK Success

85

Cute as a Button Tag

SUPPLIES

Tag - Sizzix (modified)
Sticker letters - Alphabitties, Provo Craft
Buttons - Dress it Up
Fibers - Adornaments, EK Success
Wire - Westrim Crafts

Disney Days Tag

SUPPLIES

Tag, balloons, brads, and vellum -
    Sophi-ti-cuts, Cut-it-Up
Sticker letters - SEI
Wire - Making Memories
Alphabet beads - Darice
Ribbon - Local craft store
Paper raffia - American Tag Co.

Apples Tag

SUPPLIES

Tag, apples, barrel, and brads -
    Sophis-ti-cuts, Cut-it-Up
Fibers - Creative Imaginations
Twistel - Making Memories
Ribbon - Local craft store
Chalk - Craf-T Products
Pen - Zig Writer, EK Success

Cherish, Love Tag

SUPPLIES

Tag - Sizzix
Paper - The Paper Company
Letter stamps - rubbertrouble.com
Metal letters and word - Making Memories
Fiber - Adornaments, EK Success
Pen - Zig Writer, EK Success

Ocean Waves Tag

SUPPLIES

Tag - Gift tag #4, Accu-cut
Circle tags - kI Memories
Cardstock - Monochromatics, Bazzill Basics Paper
Sticker words - Wonderful Words, Deja Views
Sand Dollars and Star Fish - Magic Scraps
Fibers - Creative Imaginations
MDC Floss - Local craft dtore
Chalk - Craft-T Products

Boys Only

SUPPLIES

Tag - Sizzix
Metal tag - Making Memories
Pattern paper - Making Memories
Sticker letters - Making Memories
Frog - My Minds Eye, Inc.
Fibers - Magic Scraps
Pop dots - All Night Media
Font - CK Kiddo

Carolyn Holt

Carolyn Holt is a well-known artist throughout the scrapbooking and rubberstamping marketplace as an inspiring teacher. Her paper crafting projects and scrapbook pages are seen in magazines and books regularly and her style has been admired for years. She has a beautiful scrapbook paper and sticker collection available through NRN Designs.

Carolyn lives happily with her husband and two young sons in Yorba Linda, California and occasionally teaches classes at local stamp and scrapbooking stores.

Beach Special

SUPPLIES

Tags, Pattern paper, Stickers, and
Photo corners - Carolyn Holt Collection,
Cardstocks - both from NRN Designs
Charms and Page pebbles - Making Memories
Shells - U.S. Shell Inc.
Wire ribbon - Offray
Shell Charm - Embellish It
Twine - Printworks
Seahorse charm - Card Connection

Carolyn's page is very unique with the way she made the pale blue pockets for the tags to slide in and out of. The square windows allow you to still view those cute faces on the tags.

Nothing is Scary

SUPPLIES

Tags, Pattern paper, Stickers and
   Photo corners - Carolyn Holt
   Collection, NRN Designs
Cardstock - NRN Designs
Vellum - NRN Designs
Fibers - Fibers by the Yard
Eyelets - Limited Edition
Pigmented inks - Colorbox, Clearsnap

Jordyn and Timmy
at the Beach

SUPPLIES

Tags, Pattern paper, Stickers and Photo corners -
   Carolyn Holt Collection, NRN Designs
Brads - Limited Edition
Fibers - Fibers by the Yard
Metal letters and Page pebbles -
   Making Memories

89

Various Artists

In the following section, these artists are just as spectacular as all of our other featured artists. They have the talent and skills to become well known scrapbooking artists. These artists have different techniques and styles that have inspired us in many ways. This may be only the beginning for many of them and we hope that they will have continued success and inspiration to keep creating all of those wonderful and memorable scrapbook pages.

Live Out Loud
by Mecque Leonard

SUPPLIES

Tags, Pattern paper, Stickers and
    Photo corners - Carolyn Holt Collection,
    NRN Designs
Fibers - Fibers by the Yard
Eyelet - alltheextras.com
Glitter - Sparkle, Personal Stamp Exchange
Shaved Ice - Magic Scraps
Font - Unknown

Simply Lovely Tag
by Linda Porter Jones

SUPPLIES

Tag - Tag Template, Deluxe Cuts
Pattern paper - Pamela Woods,
    Creative Imaginations
Metal frame and clip -
    Making Memories
Fibers - Unknown
Ink - Colorbox, Clearsnaop
Font - Linda's handwriting

Sweet, Sensitive, Silly Tag
by Laura Archuleta

SUPPLIES

Tag - Avery
Pattern paper - Dena Designs
Slide mount - Foofala
Metal flowers - Ting-a-Lings,
    Carolees Creations
Alphabet charms -
    Making Memories
Metal spring and jump ring -
    Westrim Crafts
Elastic - 7 Gypsies
Cheese cloth and organza ribbon -
    Local craft store
Letter stamps - Unknown
Paint - Colors by Plaid
Date stamp - Local office supply store

Bubble Bath
by Tara Stevenson

SUPPLIES

Tags - American Tag Co.
Pattern paper - Hot off the Press
Letters, bubbles, letters, and
    bath scene - Designed by Tara
Vellum - Golden Oak Paper
DMC floss - Local craft store
Pen - Zig Writer, EK Success
Chalk - Craf-T Products
Font - Unknown

Chad was a water baby! Mom always bathed chad in the kitchen sink, until he finally discovered the bath tub.

Garden Work
By Tara Stevenson

SUPPLIES

Tags - American Tag Co.; Pattern paper - Picture Perfect; Flowers, and letters - Designed by Tara; Wire - Westrim Crafts; Chalk - Craf-T Products; Pen - Zig Writer, EK Success

Key to my Heart Tag
by Stephanie Rarick

SUPPLIES

Tag - Designed by Stephanie in a class by Kori Babb
    at Lofty Creations
Pattern paper - Scrap-Ease
Burlap and gingham ribbon - Local craft store
Antique key - unknown
Letters - Unknown
Brads - American Tag Co.
Heart- Cut out by hand
Pen - Pigma Micron, Sakura
Jute - Local craft store
Music notes are sheet music scanned,
shrunk and walnut inked.

Family Time
by Stephanie Rarick

SUPPLIES

Tag - By Stephanie from a class by Kori Babb at Lofty
Creations; Pattern paper - Scrap-Ease and 7 Gypsies;
Shimmer and micro waffle cardstock - Unknown;
Letters - Hot off the Press; Sticker letters - Foofala;
Cork paper - Magic Scraps; Clock face – unknown; Copper
sheets - Making Memories; Brads - American Tag Co.;
Stamp & ink - unknown; Fibers - Memoriesoftherabbit.com;
Metallic Rub –Ons – Craf-T Products
Hint - Stephanie used sandpaper to give
    part of the tag an aged look.

Exit Glacier
by Stephanie Rarick

SUPPLIES

Tag - Designed by Stephanie in a class by Michelle Baker
    at Lofty Creations
Pattern paper and vellum - Scrapbook Interiors, Chatterbox
Brads and eyelet - American Tag Co.
Metal chain - Making Memories
Mesh - Magic Mesh
Letter stamps - Pixie Antique, Personal Stamp Exchange
Date stamp - Making Memories
Sticky Squares - Making Memories
Map - From local area
Pen - Pigma Micron, Sakura

Jacob
by Stephanie Rarick

SUPPLIES

Tag "look" - Designed by Stephanie
Pattern paper - Scrapbook Interiors, Chatterbox
Letter tiles - Scrabble game pieces
Brads - American Tag Co.
Page pebbles - Making Memories
Quote - Quick Quotes
Overall straps - From a pair of her son's overalls
Chalk - Craf-T Products
Hint - Stephanie sewed the edges of
   her pages and her vellum strip. Also,
   notice how she chalked certain words
   of importance.

Jacob the Kid Tag
by Stephanie Rarick

SUPPLIES

Tag - Designed by Stephanie
Pattern paper - SEI and unknown
Sticker letters - Foofala
Bandana - Jolee's by You, EK Success
Metal corners - Making Memories
Extreme eyelets - Creative Imaginations
Letter stamps - Pixie Antique, Personal Stamp Exchange
Ribbon and fabric - Local fabric store
Pen - Pigma Micron, Sakura
Chalk - Craf-T Products

Fishing Tag
by Stephanie Rarick

SUPPLIES

Tag - Designed by Stephanie
Pattern paper - Cut-it-Up
Mesh - Magic Mesh
Cork paper - Magic Scraps
Vellum tag - Making Memories
Brads - American Tag Co.
Miniature fishing pole - Westrim Crafts
Fish - Jolee's by You, EK Success
Fishing fly - Local sporting goods store
Fibers - Memoriesoftherabbit.com
Letter stamps - Pixie Antique,
   Personal Stamp Exchange;
Pen - Pigma Micron, Sakura

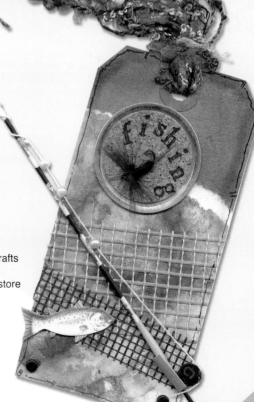

Welcome Baby Tag
by Jennifer Archuleta

SUPPLIES

Tag - Sizzix
Pattern paper - Doodlebug Design Inc.
Sticker letters - Sonnets, Creative Imaginations
Page pebbles - Making Memories
Letter stamps - rubbertrouble.com
Ribbon - Local craft store

Pitter Patter Tag
by Laura Teel

SUPPLIES

Tag - Designed by Laura
Pattern paper - Lasting Impressions
Cardstock - Monochromatics, Bazzill Basics Paper
Silver letters - Conchos, Scrapworks
Sticker letters - SEI
Metal feet - Senti-metals, Lasting Impressions
Ribbon - Local craft store
Chalk - Craf-T Products

Happy Birthday Tag
by Kylee Desuacido

SUPPLIES

Shaker Box Tag - Designed by Kylee
Maruyama - Magenta
Present - QuicKutz
Balloon punch - Punch Bunch
Shaved Ice - Magic Scraps
Eyelet - American Tag Co.
Tiny silver cording - Printworks
Fibers - Stitches, Making Memories
Pop dots - All Night Media
Font - CK Cute
Hint - Kylee used her left over pop dot
remains to make her shaker box.

Summer Dreams 2003
by Sandra Ott

SUPPLIES

Tag - Designed by Sandra
Pattern paper - NRN Designs
Palm tree and shell - QuicKutz
Vellum - Bazzill Basics Paper
Twistel - Making Memories
Eyelet - American Tag Co.
Micro beads - Magic Scraps
Chalk - Craf-T Products

It's a Jungle out There
by Mychael Rodriguez

SUPPLIES

Tag - Designed by Mychael
Pattern paper - Karen Foster Designs
Vellum - Bazzill Basics Paper
Toucan - Jolee's by You
Eyelet and paper raffia -
   American Tag Co.
Stamp - Personal Stamp
   Exchange
Chalk - Craf-T Products
Pen - Zig Writer, EK Success
Font - CK Artisan

May Flowers
by Cathleen Vincent

SUPPLIES

Tag - Designed by Cathleen; Sticker letters - SEI;
Flowers and brads - Ting-a-lings, Carolees Creations;
May sign - License Plates, Junkitz;
Fibers and Twistel - Making Memories; Chalk - Craf-T Products

4th of July

by Cathleen Vincent

SUPPLIES

Tag - Designed by Cathleen
Pattern paper - The Paper Patch
July - License Plate, Junkitz
Number four - Marisa, QuicKutz
Alphabet beads - Darice
Wire - Westrim Crafts
Star punch - Emaginations

Bon Voyage Tag

by Laura Teel

SUPPLIES

Tags Create-a-Cut
Pattern paper and Maruyama - Magenta
Stickers - Nostalgiques by Rebecca Sower,
   EK Success
Keys - Jolee's by You, EK Success
Bradwear - Creative Imaginations
Brads - Carolees Creations
Ribbon and twine - Local craft store

Home of the Free Tag

by Laura Teel

SUPPLIES

Tag - Designed by Laura; Maruyama - Magenta
Heart die cut - Sophis-ti-cuts, Cut-it-Up; Alphabet beads - Darice
Wire - Westrim Crafts; Twistel - Making Memories
Twine - Local craft store; Pen - Zig Writer, EK Success